T0279389

DRIVING MARILYN

DRIVING MARILYN

The Life and Times of
Legendary Hollywood Agent Norman Brokaw

JOEL BROKAW

FOREWORD BY DAVID GEFFEN

Essex, Connecticut

An imprint of
The Globe Pequot Publishing Group, Inc.
64 South Main Street
Essex, Connecticut 06426
www.globepequot.com

Distributed by NATIONAL BOOK NETWORK

Copyright © 2024 by Joel Brokaw
Foreword © 2024 by David Geffen
All photos courtesy of the author unless indicated otherwise

All rights reserved. No part of this book may be reproduced in any form or by any electronic or mechanical means, including information storage and retrieval systems, without written permission from the publisher, except by a reviewer who may quote passages in a review.

British Library Cataloguing in Publication Information available

Library of Congress Cataloging-in-Publication Data available
ISBN 978-1-4930-8593-4 (paper: alk. paper)
ISBN 978-1-4930-8594-1 (electronic)

♾️™ The paper used in this publication meets the minimum requirements of American National Standard for Information Sciences—Permanence of Paper for Printed Library Materials, ANSI/NISO Z39.48-1992.

To those who are encountering Norman for the first time, I hope you will be captivated and inspired by his remarkable life and times.

To all who knew Norman, I hope this will remind you of all the special times you had with him and fill in some of the backstory you perhaps never knew.

Last but not least, to his grandchildren—Alexa, Drew, Nicholas, Julia, and Oliver—Norman has left you a wonderful legacy that you are all emulating in your own distinctive ways.

CONTENTS

Foreword x

    by David Geffen

CHAPTER 1: Silver Frames 1

CHAPTER 2: Velvet and Lace 7

CHAPTER 3: Paradise Lost 15

CHAPTER 4: Opportunity Knocks 23

CHAPTER 5: The "Demotion" 31

CHAPTER 6: Big Stars and the Small Screen 37

CHAPTER 7: Marilyn and Norman Eat Dinner 45

CHAPTER 8: Kim Novak's Big Brother 53

CHAPTER 9: The Man They Called "The Colonel" 59

CHAPTER 10: Monkey Business 69

CHAPTER 11: Behind Closed Doors 75

CHAPTER 12: Exclamation Points! 85

CHAPTER 13: Hillcrest 91

CHAPTER 14: Son of a Gun 95

CHAPTER 15: Welcome to the Big Leagues 101

CHAPTER 16: Mailroom Melodrama 107

CHAPTER 17: Vick Place 113

CHAPTER 18: Secrets 121

Contents

CHAPTER 19: A Dog's Good Judgment 125

CHAPTER 20: The Agent They Let into the Oval Office 131

CHAPTER 21: The Prism 141

CHAPTER 22: Speechless 145

CHAPTER 23: The High-Wire Act 149

CHAPTER 24: "The Coach" Becomes "The Hornet" 153

CHAPTER 25: Don't Touch the Hair 161

CHAPTER 26: Genius Loves Company 169

CHAPTER 27: The Changing of the Guard 175

CHAPTER 28: The Rolodex 183

Index 189

Acknowledgments 199

I have never known anyone who was so eager, so interested, or so positive.

—KIM NOVAK

Foreword

by David Geffen

It may have just been just a job for Norman Brokaw when he joined the mailroom at William Morris—but because of him and his vision, he paved the way for so many of us. He was a pioneer.

Norman's success had many facets; the most valuable was the importance of nurturing relationships. You only needed to watch to understand why many of his clients stayed with him for decades. He made a difference in people's lives because he believed in talent and invested in us, whether we were entry-level or accomplished. He always looked for ways to be of help with joy and enthusiasm, expecting nothing in return. That was only part of the reason he rose from the mailroom to the boardroom and remained at the same company for over sixty years.

Norman is a pioneer because he recognized opportunities and wasn't afraid to explore possibilities that none of his colleagues had previously dared pursue. His early mentors saw his creativity and encouraged him; it emboldened him to not be limited by conventional thinking in how to best serve his clients, his company, and, consequently, the entertainment industry.

Norman was the last of a dying breed, but his way of free thinking, loyalty, and care for others has value. With his story we have one more chance to learn from a pioneer.

CHAPTER 1

Silver Frames

IN JULY 1943 A SIXTEEN-YEAR-OLD BOY NAMED NORMAN BROKAW bought himself a necktie, a couple of white shirts, and a dress suit to be paid off in installments. Multiple tragedies had struck his family, and new responsibilities now fell on his shoulders. So he prepared himself to take advantage of an exceptional opportunity: to become the very first mail-room trainee for the West Coast William Morris Agency office, a place where so many legendary Hollywood moguls would later get their start. It would be the very last job interview he would ever do.

Much of what came to be known as American popular culture had its epicenter at William Morris, and Norman's fingerprints can be found on most of it during the second half of the twentieth century. "So why haven't we heard of him before," many people might ask. The simple answer is that it was the way he liked it. Being famous was solely for those he represented. Self-promotion served only one in-house purpose for him: to reinforce to clients new and old that they had made the right choice in entrusting him with their careers. Throughout the decades, he had many offers for more lucrative and powerful positions in the industry (including heading a major film studio) but always declined. He truly loved being an agent, and his clients and coworkers were cherished family. He could have excelled as a salesman of any commodity, but nothing was as exciting and fulfilling to him as nurturing the talent in people.

Kim Novak was not alone in seeing something special in this dark-haired, tanned, well-groomed and enthusiastic young man who stood five feet, five inches tall in his dress shoes. The others included

Norman at entry level, eager and enthusiastic

Marilyn Monroe, Elvis, Natalie Wood, Loretta Young, Clint Eastwood, Danny Thomas, Barbara Stanwyck, Dick Van Dyke, Susan Hayward, Berry Gordy, Bill Cosby, Donna Summer, Brooke Shields, plus many more. With the emergence of broadcast television as the most powerful medium of the twentieth century, Norman's pioneering role was a showcase of his own artistry and creativity. And he singlehandedly pioneered agency representation of politicians and athletes when he signed up President Gerald Ford and his family as they were exiting the White House and Olympic champion swimmer Mark Spitz fresh from his seven gold medals in the Munich games.

"He was agent, manager, accountant, lawyer, bookkeeper, psychiatrist, all of those things," explained legendary producer George Schlatter, creator of *Rowan & Martin's Laugh-In*, the most popular television show in America in the late 1960s. "The door was always open, and you walked in there with a problem and usually came out with an answer."

Toward the tail end of his career, Norman hardly had to open his mouth for any visitor to understand that he was a person of accomplishment. His office did all the talking. Photographs mounted on the walls or placed on tabletops could tell his story much faster than any spoken word. Whether they were of Hollywood's top leading ladies or men or presidents of the United States, many were personally inscribed with messages of gratitude and appreciation. In addition, there were personal letters and newspaper articles that offered more details if the visitor had the time to study them. Most were adorned with silver frames to give equal weight and prominence to their contents.

Behind every good joke there often lurks a hidden truth if one looks hard enough. Such was the nature of one of the objects on display in Norman's welcoming and tastefully decorated office. On one of the tabletops was a hardbound book. On its glossy dust jacket was a portrait of Norman, in bold letters was written the title, *A Talent for People*, and, below that, his name as author.

Sometimes people flaunt their success because of a deep down, hidden insecurity. This was not the case with Norman. He was completely comfortable in his own skin. But appearances mattered to him. Being impeccably well dressed and having a well-appointed office served a

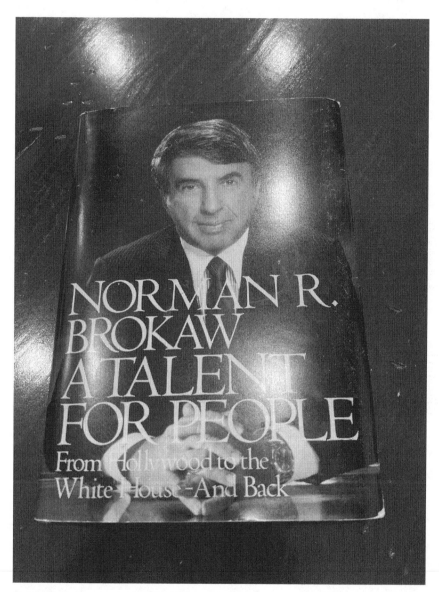

NORMAN R. BROKAW
A TALENT
FOR PEOPLE
From Hollywood to the
White House—And Back

The book that was not meant to be

higher purpose: Important people wanted their affairs to be handled by someone of equal bearing.

Beyond the exteriors, Norman had a natural sense of curiosity. Whether you were a client or just an average passerby, he wanted to get your story. True to the title of the book, he could smell talent in anyone within thirty seconds, and he knew from lifelong experience how small gestures of encouragement could lead to greater things. His enthusiasm, sincerity, positive thinking, and passion could be infectious.

One day, one of his younger colleagues, Adam Novak, was waiting in his office to follow up on a matter with him. As Norman finished a call, Adam noticed *A Talent for People* on the table. It was in his hands as Norman turned to speak with him.

"Mr. Brokaw, how come all the pages in this book are blank?"

"The book came from Warner Books. They wanted me to fill in those blank pages for seven figures. I turned them down."

"You turned them down?"

"That's right. I told Warner Books, 'My story is *still* being written!'"

As good pranks often get repeated, Norman got a laugh out of the perplexed looks on people's faces when they opened that book, according to his longtime assistant, Mary Feinberg.

The reality was that the publisher could have offered him eight figures and the pages would have remained blank. He had many stories to tell, but sharing them felt like a betrayal of trust. And God forbid there should be any pressure by the publisher to air gossip and dirty laundry to promote book sales. Norman placed all his clients, whether superstars or not, on a high pedestal. There was no payday high enough to throw anyone under the bus.

Repeated encouragement from others finally led to the day a decade later, in the mid-2000s, when he decided to start getting his story down on paper. Having me, his youngest son, help him with the process was giving him some measure of comfort. Nevertheless, he read over the few pages I had compiled for him literally dozens of times up, down, and sideways to remove any shadow of a doubt that anything negative about a client had slipped through. Mary Feinberg could not recall more than a handful of times he had said something bad about a client over the decades she worked for him. And it was understood that it was completely off-the-record and not to go further.

In our taped interviews, Norman proved to be a great storyteller but a highly reluctant one. But it was painfully clear that we had started the process too late. I had asked him to elaborate on an incident he had told me some time before. He no longer had any memory of it. The storyteller was falling silent, but the story still begged to be told.

CHAPTER 2

Velvet and Lace

ONE CONSTANT IN ALL THE HOMES NORMAN LIVED IN DURING HIS LIFE was the place of prominence given to the framed portrait of his mother's family. Pictured were an adult couple and three children, all dressed in nineteenth-century ethnic peasant garb—more specifically Ukrainian in all the details, although they identified as Russian and Yiddish-speaking. The family had roots in Poltava and Kharkiv in Ukraine.

As a small child, I was completely captivated by this beautifully hand-colorized photograph. The handsome faces, the intricate laces and floral patterns on their clothing, the silky velvets, shiny leather boots, and Cossack fur hats spoke to a more exotic world than San Fernando Valley suburbia. I fantasized about traveling in a time machine to the 1890s and spending time with them.

As I grew older, this side of the family continued to fascinate me, wishing that I could have listened to their stories from their lips. The only one I knew was my grandmother Marie, but my memories are very hazy, as she died when I was about four years old. Norman was no great help in retrieving family history for reasons not entirely his own fault. As was customary during that time, many new immigrants wanted their children to become assimilated Americans as quickly as possible, so the language and culture of the Old Country and corresponding personal history were not eagerly passed down. Anti-Semitism and the deadly pogroms of Russia and Eastern Europe they were escaping make this intention more understandable.

7

The Hydes: Rosa and Nicholas with children Victor, Nettie, and Marie

When this part of the family (including three additional children not pictured in the portrait) stepped off the boat from Hamburg onto the docks in Philadelphia in 1898, they were hardly peasants. The rustic clothing was not their everyday wear but stage wardrobe they donned while performing at the top theaters in Europe—and the aforementioned photo was no doubt used to promote their appearances. Norman's mother, Marie, his uncle Johnny, along with their sisters, Nettie and Olga, brothers, Alex and Victor, and their parents, Nicholas and Rosa, soon gained notoriety as the first Russian acrobatic dance troupe to appear on the American vaudeville stage. An article in the *Boston Herald* referred to them as "The Imperial Russian Troupe of dancers," reporting that "The Hyde (children) were born in St. Petersburg and began dancing in public as mere children. They have appeared before the Czar of Russia, President Faure of France, King Edward, and other great ones of Europe."

Upon arrival in America, the family name was Americanized from the foreign-sounding Haidabura to Hyde. But they retained the old name professionally. Acts imported from Europe were a popular novelty at the time, and "The Haidabura Troupe" had a more exotic ring to it. A young American theatrical agent who had just opened his own company was responsible for bringing them over. His name was William Morris.

The Haidaburas were an instant success and played all the important theater circuits. A reviewer from the *Norfolk Weekly New Journal* published on January 10, 1902, wrote:

A novel and interesting feature of the entertainment given by W. S. Cleveland's "tip top" minstrel and "polite" vaudeville show this season is the act of the Haidabura family. This has been the feature of a long run at the Wintergarten, Berlin, and the Folies Bergère, Paris, where it won great renown and much favorable notice, being new, interesting and the only kind in the world. They reproduce the fetes and dances of the lower Russias in the bright, picturesque costumes of the Russian peasants. Their vocal numbers are a revelation to the musical people of Europe and America, but it is their wonderful dancing that the most commend them to notice. The peculiarly pretty and graceful steps of the ladies and the wonderful dexterity and agility of the men were the sensation of the amusement season in Chicago, where they appeared in conjunction with the Cleveland shows. Mr. Cleveland's European representative secured a long contract with this great act and being under his exclusive management and the only act of the kind in the world. it will never be seen in America excepting in connection with one of his shows.

Time marched on, and with the children all grown up, Nicholas disbanded the troupe in 1914. Some of them continued in various aspects of the performing arts. Forming a duo with Nettie, Victor later became a producer and impresario of vaudeville and circus acts, as well as a teacher of Russian dance. Alex was regarded as a highly accomplished violinist and bandleader. Under the umbrella of Paul Whiteman, the Alex Hyde Orchestra played a major part in the wave of the popularization of jazz as a serious art form. They were a sensation in America and Europe (including Berlin's cabaret scene) in the 1920s and recorded on Deutsche Grammophon. Later, he put together the first all-female jazz orchestra, much like what was later portrayed in the film *Some Like It Hot*. Since he spoke German, Alex was also hired by the Hollywood film studios in the early 1940s as a liaison to help refugee German film composers (like Franz Waxman and Erich Korngold) escaping from the Nazis adjust to life in America and integrate into the industry.

Thanks to Marie, Johnny Hyde got a job on the business end of show business as an assistant booking manager of the Loews Vaudeville Circuit. As a child, Marie had learned English the fastest and consequently managed a lot of the bookings for the troupe. Those long-standing connections with the agencies made it possible to get her brother the job.

Years later, he rose to the top and ran the William Morris talent agency alongside Norman's later mentor, Abe Lastfogel, working at the very company that had brought him to America as a child. When he first started out there, he represented the top stage attractions of the day: Al Jolson, Eddie Cantor, the Marx Brothers, the Ritz Brothers, and George Jessel. As Hollywood movies and radio took precedence over live vaudeville theater, he moved west from New York to head the Beverly Hills office. His stellar client list included Mae West, Bob Hope, Lana Turner, Rita Hayworth, Betty Hutton, Mickey Rooney, Amos 'n Andy, Tallulah Bankhead, Linda Darnell, and other A-listers of that era. Without question, what made Johnny Hyde a great agent was a product of his upbringing in a show business family—and the same can later be said for Norman.

While her brothers continued to work in show business, Marie got married and preceded to have seven children: six boys, of whom Norman was the youngest, and one daughter, who died in infancy. Her husband, Isidore Brokaw, was also Russian-born, a lawyer by profession who made a fortune in real estate in New York in the 1920s.

The Brokaws (or Avreshcovs, as they were called in the old country) had arrived in New York from Odessa and Bobrynets around 1890, when Isidore was around four years old. His parents, David and Rose Brokaw, produced a total of nine children: four boys and five girls. They were more of an average Jewish immigrant family than were the famous Haidaburas, hardworking people who applied their trade as milliners who made and sold hats on 38th Street in New York. As the years went on, they prospered from owning their own businesses.

Isidore was the only member of the Brokaw family to become truly wealthy. In 1929 his estate was said to be worth about $2 million; the equivalent value nearly a hundred years later would be at least $60 million (some comparison indexes go as high as $100 million). He had sizable property holdings and maintained a large office with lawyers, real estate managers, and insurance people working for him.

On Sundays he would send his chauffeured limousine to pick up one of his brothers or sisters and their spouses to go out to dinner and see the new bill at the Palace Theater. That side of the family was very tightly knit. With Isidore as the lone exception, the Brokaw brothers and sisters would pack up their respective children each summer for six weeks to escape the heat of the city, staying at a Catskill Mountains resort or a hotel at the beach in Far Rockaway. The men would take the train up from the city on Friday and return to the run their businesses on Monday.

Isidore did not need to go on those summer trips because the life he created for his family in Larchmont, New York, was as good if not better than any resort. Sixteen-millimeter home movies from the late 1920s document the family's enclave of privilege. The films show a large gabled manor home with spacious gardens. Luxury automobiles driven by the parents and their older kids are seen coming and going. Isidore is shown returning from work in his suit and tie and overcoat with a velvet collar. Rolling up his shirtsleeves, he is quickly recruited for a game of touch football on the massive lawn. Marie drives up in her Lincoln sedan, dressed elegantly in a flapper-style hat, frock dress, and expensive jewelry. A governess hands Norman over to her, and he sits for a moment on her lap, grabbing the steering wheel. Several months later he is shown as a two-year-old holding a golf putter and playing on the backyard miniature golf course. In that same film roll, he is filmed discreetly urinating on the trunk of a tree.

Other clips show the oldest brother, Sidney, an accomplished violinist, clowning like a slapstick comedian at the beach and flirting with the bathing beauty flappers with his fellow band members (who would all soon be well known as the Ozzie Nelson Orchestra). There's footage of the next-oldest brother, Irving, graduating from the New York Military Academy at Cornwall-on-Hudson in full dress uniform. Another brother, the teenaged Donnie, wearing one of those old-fashioned tank-top bathing suits, executes a perfect dive off a high board into the swimming pool. Dinnertime, attended to by cook and maid, shows Isidore at the head of the large family table eating in an elegant but somewhat self-conscious manner, knowing that the newfangled film camera was focused on him.

Norman's parents had met as teenagers and were married when his father was twenty-two and his mother was eighteen. From large families on both sides, they quickly had five boys. My mother wished for a girl, and on the sixth attempt got what she wanted; she declared she was done with childbearing, or so she thought. One day she went into the city to do some shopping and left her infant daughter, Barbara, in the care of the governess. It was a sunny but cold winter day. The governess wanted to take her lunch break and considered taking the baby upstairs to the sunroom to nap. Instead, she bundled the baby up in the carriage and took her outside to the garden. She used some ribbons to tie the baby's hands down for a few minutes until she returned from her break, probably to prevent the baby from lifting herself and falling out of the carriage. But when the governess came back out, the baby was lying lifeless in her carriage. Apparently, she had tried to turn and had strangled herself in a tangle of ribbons and blankets. Marie returned from her shopping trip to

Marie Brokaw and her sons (seated left to right: Lenny, Marie, Norman, Eddie, and Sidney; standing left to right: Donnie and Irving)

a devastating tragedy. On April 21, 1927, Norman was born—an attempt to restore joy to a grieving family.

The details of Barbara's tragic death were not common knowledge to Norman, or so it appeared. The truth came out when my father put me in touch with his older cousin Mildred Libby (from the Brokaw side) as part of the research for his aborted memoir. She was seven years older than he, and although she was well into her nineties when I phoned her, her memory was sharp as a tack; she spoke with such vivid detail, like it all had happened yesterday. After our conversation, I had to break the news to Norman that Barbara's passing was not a case of sudden infant death syndrome, as had long been assumed, but a horrible accident. Mildred recalled how devastated Marie was and how Isidore, who had a delightful and happy personality, was never the same person afterward. Naturally, such a horribly painful event was rarely if ever spoken about again in the family. So it was news to Norman when I told him about it some eighty years after the fact.

I thought he might become emotional, since it was the event responsible for his very conception. But he was silent and pensive for a few seconds. "Huh, isn't that something," he finally said. It will always be a mystery to me what he was thinking. Maybe it wasn't such a surprise to him. Given how generally tightlipped he was about his childhood, he possibly knew all along but didn't want to let on, but that's anyone's guess. Perhaps it was the elder's voice of reason of someone who had seen it all, resigned to such tragedies as a fact of life.

CHAPTER 3

Paradise Lost

How tempting it is to look back at pivotal moments early on in
a life and conclude that the die was cast. We all want logical explana-
tions behind our patterns of behavior and resulting actions. Some of the
answers can be so blaringly simple, staring us right in the face, while
others are convoluted enigmas that will never be solved. We want things
to make sense, for all the dots to be conveniently connected, so we can
come a little closer to justifying our place in a chaotic world.

The conversation I had with Mildred was insightful not only for the
facts she revealed but also for something more qualitative. There was no
one else left on the planet who could tell me what Norman was like as
a child. From her glowing account, he was someone who lit up a room
with his presence—a beloved, happy, and fun kid. There is not much more
a child can ask for than to be adored as much as Norman was. True, he
was a replacement and carried the emotional charge of his parents' recent
trauma, a projection of their gratitude and natural phobia of history
repeating itself. And being the last of the large litter, he basked in being
the center of attention, demonstrated so vividly in those home movies
shot in the late 1920s and early 1930s. As he grew older, Norman loved
going on outings with his father, especially to Coney Island, either to
Feltman's (the inventor of the hot dog) or its upstart competitor, Nathan's.

Slowly but surely, Norman's seemingly carefree life imploded. The
first blow came early. The paradise-like idyll so evident in the home
movies proved to be as unstable as the decaying nitrate stock of the original footage on which it was shot. With the stock market crash of 1929,

Isidore's great wealth began to wither away. The house in Larchmont was soon gone, as were all the automobiles, the serving staff, and all the other trappings of luxury that coddled Norman as an infant. The family moved to an apartment in Manhattan at 949 West End Avenue.

It wasn't all gloom. During the mid-1930s Norman still took piano lessons from a teacher in a nearby apartment building. It was part of the family culture that when company came, someone would say, "Let's have a song," and the youngest child would be expected to play. With the piano lessons, his prowess as a dealmaker was already starting to show itself. He purposely got Marie to time the lesson with another event. It must have looked strange to see him going off to a piano lesson with a baseball glove and ball in hand. At that hour, afternoon games at Yankee Stadium would usually be over and the piano teacher's neighbor would be coming home. The person Norman would ask to play catch with him first called him "Sonny," but as it became a repeat ritual, he would soon call him "Normie." The man was Lou Gehrig.

Norman also honed his craft at school at PS 54. He convinced his teacher and the principal that it was a Jewish holiday and that he should be excused from school for observance. He was so convincing that he told the rest of the kids to take the day off too, which they did. The thrill of that successful negotiation was short-lived once his deception was uncovered and he was punished.

To help the family, he got a job at the Pennsylvania Drug Company in New York, delivering prescriptions for a nickel a piece. His mother came into the store one day and saw that he was wrapping a box of Kotex. She prudishly told his boss, "He's too young to be doing that!" On a good week, he made ten dollars, which he handed over to his mother. He also made some money taking back milk drink bottles to the grocery store for deposit. With that change, he would go on his own to the Riverside Theatre to see the talent shows on Sunday afternoon. He saw Ella Fitzgerald sing her big breakthrough hit song "A-Tisket, A-Tasket" with the Chuck Webb Orchestra at the Loews State Theater on Broadway and Mickey Rooney or Judy Garland over at the Strand. He might have been only eleven years old or so, but he made up his mind that this was where he wanted to be—far more exciting than what the retail drugstore business had to offer.

Marie started her own business, the Ladies Athletic Club, at the Park Central Hotel, a health spa and gym that was certainly ahead of its time. A lot of show business celebrities like Sophie Tucker and Fanny Brice, who she encountered when she was a performer years earlier, were her clients. She was working there in the summer of 1940 when she got the phone call that Isidore had suffered a heart attack. Norman was down in Atlantic City visiting his brother Eddie, who had a summer job on the Boardwalk. He was staying with him on a pull-out bed in a basement room that was as tiny as a jail cell. They got the phone call and rushed home. Two days later, Isidore passed away at age fifty-five. Cardiovascular disease ran in both sides of the family, and tobacco use along with generally unhealthy diets didn't help matters. Mildred speculated that the grief over Barbara's death played a far larger part in Isidore's decline than the stress over the family's lost fortune. Marie sold her last piece of jewelry to pay for the funeral. Norman was fourteen years old and devastated.

Norman's first job, at the Pennsylvania Drug Company

Isidore Brokaw

In August of 1941, his second-oldest brother, Irving, was called up as an officer in the reserves and sent to the Philippines. The army thought that since he had been a rich man's son, he was the perfect person to serve with Gen. Douglas MacArthur and train Philippine bankers, lawyers, and doctors to become officers in their army. Four months later, the Japanese bombed Pearl Harbor and the war came quickly to the Philippines. The US soldiers stationed there were essentially hung out to dry—undermanned, under-resourced, and too far away for the supplies and reinforcements so urgently needed to arrive in time.

Not much is left to the imagination about what Irving went through, thanks to some letters he wrote to his wife in February of 1942 that somehow made it out of the war zone. Blow by blow, they describe the overwhelming stress of being overrun by the Japanese. A month earlier, he had received a Silver Star for withstanding a tank attack and leading his men to safety in the swamps. He told his wife proudly that he had been recommended for promotion from lieutenant to captain.

"At Malilao, I was camp commander. When the war broke out here on December 8 [1941], the Japs were already here. I looked out on Ligayon [sic] Gulf and saw an array of troop and supply ships like so many toy boats in a swimming pool. I counted 36 in view. At first, they stayed about a mile offshore, but several days later, they began to come in close. A battery of 75's was attached to me and I used them almost daily to keep the ships as far from shore as possible. The Jap bombers constantly dropped their eggs on my camp, reduced it to ashes."

(*Note:* The word "Jap" was in common use before and during World War II but is considered a racial slur. It is reprinted here only for historical accuracy.)

Things went from bad to worse as the base he was defending fell, forcing a harrowing retreat into the swamps and jungle. "From Betis we withdrew to Guagua. I was in my command post about 100 yards behind the line and was suddenly surrounded by Japs. I shot my way out of that, crossed a stream while still exposed to Jap tommy-gun fire for a full five minutes, and had the most miraculous escape possible. Even I cannot explain why the streams of lead pouring at me failed to find my back. When I finally reached the swamps, I came upon a group of my men, including four Filipino officers. I lead them through the difficult terrain until we came to a river. There was no way to cross except by swimming. The damned river was only about 150 yards wide, but when I got to the middle of it both my thighs cramped, and I began to sink. Three of my men saved my life. [A doctor] told me that the paralysis of the legs after such a strain as I had undergone was quite a normal reaction. You see, I had walked through river and swamp mud almost hip high. The suction in this mud is so strong that it requires a tremendous amount of strength to pull the legs free. I crossed about seven more rivers during that night, but all by banca [a Philippine dugout canoe]. The next morning, I got a native to paddle the whole detachment to Orani. It was a two-and-a-half-hour ride and a tremendous relief to know that I was getting out of the ponds and swamps and free from being trapped by the Japs."

Irving goes on to write to his wife. "Now we are in dense jungle. Our main hope is for aid from the States. As a matter of fact, it is our only hope. Somehow, I feel that this will end up all right and that I will get back to you safely."

Norman came into the kitchen one day after work and found his mother lying on the floor. She was holding a telegram informing her that Irving was missing in action. She had collapsed with a heart attack from the shock. His death would be confirmed four years later, indicating that he had been captured in the fall of Corregidor and presumed to have perished in the infamous Death March of Bataan. The Japanese had forced the prisoners of war to march ninety miles without food and water for over a week in the tropical heat. Survivors told of the horrors: Anyone who couldn't keep up, who tried to help a struggling comrade, or who simply protested was shot, beheaded, or had their throat cut. Losing a big brother on top of his father, both of whom he idolized, was an intense sorrow Norman would carry for the rest of his life.

Not long after getting the news, three of his four remaining brothers joined the military to avenge Irving's death, one in each branch of service. His oldest brother, Sidney, was thirty-three years old with three children and exempted from service. The draft board told Norman that he was too young to enlist, although he did end up serving a few weeks in the army at Fort MacArthur in Los Angeles Harbor in the last months of the war. Marie recovered from her heart attack, checked out of the hospital, and got right onto the train to California with Norman while she was still dressed in her sickroom pajamas. She wanted to live closer to her brothers Johnny and Alex and to her sons, who were training on the West Coast and would soon be shipped off to fight in the Pacific.

It is a strange irony that some months before, Norman had gone through the Jewish ritual of the Bar Mitzvah, the last joyful vestige of his formerly carefree life. His father was still alive at the time and was tickled that Norman was the only one of his children who had chosen to go through with it. His family was not the least religious, and Norman's motivation for doing so was hardly spiritual. He had seen how a few of his classmates had walked away with a nice collection of white envelopes stuffed with cash and thought it worth the trouble.

The harsh reality was that Norman didn't need a religious ceremony to mark his passage into manhood. By age fourteen his childhood had come to a decisively crashing halt. Carefree days were over. Playing catch or practicing the piano ceased forever. The repercussions of this jarring entry into adulthood not only sowed the seeds of success in his career to come but also would be a source of stress in his personal life.

I think I can speak for all my siblings that we felt somewhat deprived that Norman rarely shared with us anecdotes from his upbringing and youth. We almost needed a power tool to pry anything out of him. He just didn't seem to want to go there, probably for the reasons mentioned above. We got vicarious dribs and drabs in pleasant and sometimes surprising ways. Sometime in the mid-1960s, he discovered a company that delivered bottled soft drinks, so he had crates of some of the unhealthy sodas he drank as a child for us to also sample (and decay our teeth), things like cream sodas we wouldn't have tried on our own. Frozen Nathan's hot dogs from Coney Island were shipped to him. He had also loved baseball as a child and gone to games at the nearby Polo Grounds in New York, so he bought Los Angeles Dodger season tickets for my brothers and me. It proved to be a godsend for us, a healthy diversion from all the trauma at home that would soon be a sad reality.

Many years later, I happened to be on a business trip to New York at the same time as Norman. We were at an event together and took a long walk down Madison Avenue in the late evening in the direction of our nearby hotels. I don't think I had ever experienced my father as relaxed and inwardly content as in that half hour we walked. He was back in his element, as if the child from his youth on these streets, whom he had so long repressed, was welcomed back into his spirit.

CHAPTER 4

Opportunity Knocks

JULY 7, 1943, WAS A REMARKABLY FATEFUL DAY IN NORMAN BROKAW'S life. One can always speculate on how life would have panned out had the day's calendar been different. Looking back on it many decades later, the story of that day takes on epic proportions.

Although he was barely sixteen years old at the time, Norman was fully conscious of what was at stake. After all he and his family had been through, a lot rested on his shoulders. It was high time for something to go right.

It was to be a lunch meeting. Norman and his mother, Marie, pulled up to Johnny Hyde's home in the Hollywood Hills high above the Cahuenga Pass. A man of great power in the industry, Johnny could look down from his throne to see Paramount Studios and the other film and radio factories on the Hollywood side to the south and look north to the Hollywood Bowl and Warner Brothers' sprawling campus down the opposite slope toward Burbank.

Johnny Hyde was very short in stature, and the furniture in his home was somewhat scaled down to accommodate it. But he made up for that by being rather imposing in his personality. It also helped that he still had the lithe but sturdy posture of an acrobat from his performing years. Marie would always remind Norman every time they went over to Johnny's house to visit his grandmother Rosa, who lived with him, "Don't forget to say hello to your uncle." Johnny had a gruff and formal manner, and Marie warned that he would take offense if Norman didn't pay his respects.

But on that particular Thursday afternoon, Johnny was behaving very warmly toward them. He knew the losses his sister had suffered. "Would you like to work at the office?" he asked Norman. Nepotism was a tricky thing, and Johnny already had two of his sons working at the company. There were any number of cousins in the family who needed a break, but considering what his older sister had been through, he extended Norman the offer. Perhaps he also remembered the payback, since she had gotten him his first job as an agent.

Before Norman could respond, the phone rang and Johnny got up to take the call. Phones were hardly portable back then; he closed the door to a closet-like booth located in the hallway. While he was on the phone, Norman and Marie looked out the window and saw a beautiful young woman coming out of a changing room in an equally stunning white bathing suit. She dove gracefully into the swimming pool. By the time his uncle was finished with his call, so was the woman with her swim. Introductions were made. She was in town to sign a contract Johnny had gotten for her at MGM. After she said goodbye, he told them, "Just remember what I'm telling you; she's going to be a huge star." He was right. Her name was Esther Williams, the star of many films showcasing her aquatic skills. That was not the only news Johnny Hyde made that day. He also closed a deal for two Hollywood moguls, Bill Goetz and Leo Spitz, to start a new venture called International Pictures, which soon morphed into the powerhouse that became Universal Studios.

The dreamlike fantasy turned reality of the bathing beauty at the mountaintop palace of a Hollywood demigod was like the stuff made in Tinseltown just down the road. Life was imitating art. Norman must have considered it a kind of affirmation—perhaps the aspirations of that young boy who pawned milk bottles and took the streetcar to Broadway to watch the shows were coming to pass.

Norman made sure his uncle knew how grateful he was, and how much he realized it was not an offer that was easy to come by. He told him that he would work his hardest not to squander this chance. It was a feeling that never left him for the rest of his lifetime, paying forward the shot he was given by later helping countless others. "My uncle wasn't one who would say, 'Come on down; I'm going to open my doors to you,'"

Making the right impression at Uncle Johnny's home

Norman recalled. Johnny Hyde's act of kindness that day was out of the ordinary and thus had an added gravitas.

Johnny instructed his nephew to meet Sam Burke at the William Morris office in Beverly Hills at 202 North Canon Drive the following Monday. He did so and hadn't even warmed his seat before emphasizing to Burke how much he appreciated the opportunity. They talked a little bit about the family and what had just happened to his brother Irving. Formalities concluded, Burke hired him to start at $25 a week. The take-home pay after income tax was around $17 or $18, which Norman gave to his mother. He needed a suit and didn't have one, so he went down to the Thrifty Drug store and got some white dress shirts and a tie. He then walked over to Jerry Rothschild's clothing store on Beverly Drive and bought a $40 suit with two pairs of pants, which he paid off in weekly $2 installments.

Just a few days into the job, someone came into the mailroom with a package and asked him to take it to the post office a few blocks away. Handed the keys to the car, Norman trembled and thought he was going to be fired on the spot. He admitted that he didn't have his license yet but would be getting it very soon. To his relief, the person told him not to worry about it. "Miss Appel, would you mind taking Mr. Brokaw to the post office? We may have to have you help him out for a while." He hoped they were cutting him some slack because they had gotten to like him, but Johnny Hyde probably factored in. They wanted the boss to be satisfied.

From day one Norman made up his mind that he didn't want to be known as the nephew who succeeded, but rather do it all on his own. So he never mentioned the connection to Johnny to anyone to gain an advantage, even though everyone in the office knew about it. "I always did what I felt was right," Norman explained. "I used whatever I learned. Each day goes by, you learn something you didn't know the day before."

It wasn't very long before Norman had his driver's license. His first day with it, fresh out of passing the test at the DMV, his services were immediately pressed into action. He was tasked with driving Fanny Brice, the legendary comedienne and entertainer, to see a performance by a new comic named Danny Thomas. "Can't you drive faster," Brice implored.

Norman complied and was soon the recipient of his very first speeding ticket. On the way back, Brice asked again, and history repeated itself. Norman always joked that getting two speeding tickets on his very first day of driving had to be a world record.

A few months later, in January of 1944, Norman had another far more memorable driving experience on the job. He was on his way from the Beverly Hills office to the studios in Hollywood when he noticed a soldier in uniform hitchhiking. As was the custom, Norman picked him up. Making conversation, he shared with him all about his brothers in the service, especially about Irving and the more recent horrible news about his brother Eddie. Just a couple of weeks earlier, Eddie's ship, the USS *Brownson*, had been sunk by Japanese dive-bombers off the coast of New Britain in the South Pacific. Eddie was MIA. Astoundingly, the soldier told Norman that he had just returned from photographing the rescue operation for that vessel. He was going to a photo lab in Hollywood to develop the film and invited Norman to come with him. On the wet photographic paper was the evidence: Eddie on a stretcher—one of the lucky survivors.

Interestingly, the hitchhiking soldier came to be a well-known person in his own right. His name was Lloyd Shearer, better known under the nom de plume Walter Scott, gossip columnist for *Parade* magazine, read weekly at its peak by an estimated fifty million people in seven hundred newspapers.

Regardless of his lowly position at the time, Norman already had a clarity of vision and apparently did not hold back from setting his mind on bigger things. My brother Sandy recalled an encounter he had some years ago with a successful personal manager named Jan. "She told me that Norman was the first guy she ever had a date with, around 1945. I asked her what they did and she said they went for ice cream and maybe a movie. Afterward, he took her to the William Morris offices at 202 North Canon. Norman told her, 'One day I'm going to run this place.'"

Ben Holzman, one of the older agents, was the first to step up as a mentor. He represented some of the old guard, including Al Jolson, Eddie Cantor, and George Jessel. Holzman knew that Norman didn't have a father, so he stepped up in that role, taking Norman out to dinner every Monday night. Holzman recognized early on that Norman was a bit too tightly wound and needed some form of stress reduction. So he took him along on a few two-week fishing vacations in the High Sierras of California.

Norman the fisherman only lasted for several years more. He had the whole getup, including the green vest with lots of tiny pockets, some filled with small containers of lead weights and jars of nasty-smelling bait. Some weekends he would take us, his young sons, to a small pond stocked with trout at the Sportsman's Lodge on Ventura Boulevard, a few blocks from the house. He would fish while we fed popcorn we got from a small vending machine to the resident ducks. The last straw was a trip with all of us to Mammoth Mountain in the Sierras in the summer. He went out fishing the first day on Lake Mary without success. That evening, my brother David vomited all over the staircase of the A-frame

Fishing in the Sierras for stress reduction

Left–right: First person unknown, Red Skelton, Joe Louis, Harpo Marx, George Burns, Frank Sinatra, Norman, Calvin Jackson

house Norman had rented for us. The next morning, we packed up and made the long trip home. As children, we couldn't understand how David's stomach problem could possibly have ruined the whole trip; he had recovered well and, after all, we had just got there. From that point forward, the fishing equipment was retired to gather dust and cobwebs in the garage.

As time progressed, Norman graduated from trainee to junior agent but was still wearing the tread down on his tires. "I would go to the studios, pick up the checks; I would do as directed, try to be helpful, make it easy for everybody," Norman recalled. It sounded like busywork, but Norman loved it and saw a clear upside. "Being there at the studios, people would say, 'Look at how that agent is taking an interest in his client. We're on a set today. My agent didn't come by and see me like Mr. Brokaw does his people.'"

CHAPTER 5

The "Demotion"

ON A THURSDAY MORNING IN THE SPRING OF 1949, ABE LASTFOGEL told Norman that he was leaving for New York that day. "When I come back, I'll want to see you in my office on Wednesday at ten o'clock in the morning." He went on to say, "I want to talk to you about something that's going to become very important. There's no locked-in name for it yet, but it's going to be called television. One day, it will be one of the biggest parts of our business."

Had Abe Lastfogel worked in the twenty-first century, his name would be infinitely more recognizable to the world outside of his immediate industry. But that was not the way of the old world, especially not his world. There was no social media or no publicly traded William Morris stock that forced Abe Lastfogel to raise his profile or trade on his name. He was a small, cherubic man in a bow tie who delighted in his work and commanded respect from everyone due to his integrity. He was a powerful figure to whom many owed their careers, but he had no pompous airs about him. In my mind, he had more in common with the Dalai Lama than an accomplished Hollywood powerbroker—the wise guru who showed the way to his eager disciples, Norman Brokaw among them. He was addressed by all as "Mr. Lastfogel" as a sign of respect and admiration, never "Abe."

Beyond what he meant to the agency, Abe Lastfogel put aside his career during World War II to put Hollywood to work in the war effort, most notably serving as president of USO Camp Shows. He rustled up the entertainers to go into the theaters of war, visiting bases and hospitals

When Abe Lastfogel speaks . . .

and going right up to the front lines to bring cheer and show how much a grateful nation valued and appreciated their service. Not much different than vaudeville shows, the performances that Lastfogel put together had an outreach to more than two million serving in uniform. His efforts to speedily mobilize the entire entertainment industry was akin to the aircraft, auto, and other consumer products industries that shifted to ramp up production of wartime supplies. Thanks to his contributions, the USO became the largest charitable organization with outreach to men and women in the active military.

One of the classic Abe Lastfogel stories was regarding Zsa Zsa Gabor, the thick-accented Hungarian actress whose larger-than-life personality kept her in the public eye via the gossip media right to the end of her ninety-nine years. She was being represented by newly promoted agent Irv Schechter, and he had a film offer for her. He told her that he needed to go into the files to see what kind of billing and salary she had on the last project, and that he would try to increase it. She told him, "You don't have to. I want you to lie. And if you don't, I'll call Mr. Lastfogel and have you fired!" Troubled by this, Irv asked to see Mr. Lastfogel and nervously shared what happened. "You call her back and tell her we at the Morris office do not lie. And she's no longer a client."

Mr. Lastfogel was an astute judge of human character and thought it prudent to give Norman fair warning of an impending change to soften the blow. As a junior agent in the motion picture department, Norman was enjoying every minute. He was learning the business and enjoying success, covering the studios during the day and going to openings and premieres at night. Over the next four days until Mr. Lastfogel returned from New York for their meeting, his spirits were very low. He feared he was being demoted, and he felt down about it.

On Wednesday morning, while Norman was getting himself ready to go to his office, Mr. Lastfogel called him on the phone to remind him about the meeting, underscoring the important nature of what he had to present. At the appointed time, Norman walked down the hallway into the boss's office and took his usual seat facing his desk.

"I want you to start the television department," Mr. Lastfogel said without beating around the bush. "This is going to be something new, so you'll have to do it from scratch." And he wasn't kidding.

"How would you like me to proceed?"

"I leave that up to you." Gulp!

A couple of days later, a sixteen-millimeter film projector and a portable screen were dropped off to his office. Next, the company took some additional space in the garage of the building next door. A partition was built, and someone must have gotten a good deal on paint at Sears, because the walls, desks, and chairs were all given a fresh beige coat. The projector and screen were set up there to act as a screening room in order to convert hesitant and doubting stakeholders to embrace the new medium.

Norman thought it was hardly a glamorous proposition that this converted space was going to be his base of operations. While the paint dried, he scratched his head, trying to figure out how he was going to rise to Mr. Lastfogel's challenge. But, as things would rapidly unfold, it proved to be a funny twist on the classic American Dream archetype of a gigantic enterprise that started up in a garage.

As the 1940s were ending, television was still a novelty. Norman was one of the few among family, friends, and neighbors who had an actual television at home, a wooden cabinet that had a six-inch black-and-white screen. People would come over and stand around the set because the picture was too small for all to watch from the sofa.

The first television station was licensed in 1941, after the technology came to mass awareness at the 1939 New York World's Fair. Delayed by the war, it was not until 1946 that primitive local shows, mostly concentrated on the East Coast, began to be broadcast to the few who had the boxes at home. The technology soon made national broadcasting possible, and the big radio networks got into the business. Until 1950, most of what was available was sports like boxing and wrestling, game shows, news, live theater, and the big sensation of the time, the *Texaco Star Theater* variety show with Milton Berle.

"Uncle Miltie" was the first big name who had the creative vision to showcase television's great entertainment potential. He dressed in drag and played other outrageous characters. Thanks to him, TV sets started selling like hotcakes. Street traffic and restaurant business across America were down when he took to the air. The phenomenon was so huge that the Morris office later secured Milton Berle a thirty-year contract for his Tuesday-night show.

Meanwhile, back at the garage, Norman came up with an idea. He took out a pad and pencil and started compiling a list based on some very clear, hard-core realities. If TV were to be truly viable and become as popular as radio, new programming was badly needed, especially in the dramatic series genre. But at the time, this new medium was still a question mark in most people's minds. The jury was still out with actors and actresses especially. Those with successful careers in the movie business thought it too much of a risk to jump onboard. Neither did the pay offer much incentive. The entire weekly budget of the average show, both above and below the line—covering everything from salaries for the star to the electrician, renting the studio space, and the agency commissions—was $10,000 a week. And if they did the usual breakneck pace of filming three half-hour shows a week, the star might walk away with only $750 tops.

Norman started writing names on his pad, including Barbara Britton, Diana Lynn, Coleen Gray, Wanda Hendricks, and Reed Hadley. What they all had in common was that they had been important working actors in the film business with some name recognition, but things had eased up a little and they were no longer in high demand. As a first step, he would meet with them and crank up the projector as part of the presentation, giving them a sample of the kinds of opportunities that were available. He then got them under contract and put them into different shows that, as noted, paid very little, but they appreciated the work.

"He's signing cats and dogs," Bert Allenberg complained to Mr. Lastfogel, criticism that stung from a big agent who had quickly become another of his mentors when his firm merged with William Morris in 1950.

"Normie, don't pay any attention to what he's saying," Mr. Lastfogel said gently but firmly and with a slight smile on his face. "Go ahead and do what you've been doing." Not long after, Barbara Britton was starring in *Mr. and Mrs. North* and Red Hadley was headlining *Racket Squad*, both hit shows.

Signing those actors was only part of his formula. On another piece of paper, he made another list: Lou Landis. Les Goodwin. Frank Mitchell. They were film directors who were specialists in low-budget movies, what were called back then "ten day wonders." They knew how to deliver a feature-length movies in ten days, so Norman knew they could work under the tighter time and budget constraints of TV. He started signing them too, and they did very well.

Before they knew it, the company was "packaging" television series. Packaging was nothing new, since William Morris used that concept in radio shows of representing the actors, producers, writers, and director connected to the same program. They started selling weekly series like *My Little Margie, The Stu Erwin Show, Racket Squad, Public Defender,* and others. Variety shows like the *Colgate Comedy Hour, Saturday Night Review,* and *The Show of Shows* with Sid Caesar and Imogene Coca, along with Milton Berle, were also William Morris deals.

As television quickly evolved, packaging became a norm in the business. The track record the company started to build by collaborating with the networks and their advertisers gave the program buyers another layer of assurance that the finished product would be of the highest quality and delivered on time and on budget. They were well on their way.

CHAPTER 6

Big Stars and the Small Screen

THE NEXT BREAKTHROUGH WAS GETTING A MAJOR FILM STAR TO MAKE the move and headline a television series. On this front, one helpful development sweetened the pot considerably. Lucille Ball and Desi Arnaz moved their popular radio show to television, and *I Love Lucy* became a smash hit. Most importantly, they had set up their own company, Desilu Productions, to produce the show.

Bert Allenberg and Norman went over to Loretta Young's house on the corner of Laurel Avenue and Fountain just off the Sunset Strip. Loretta was without question among the highest echelon of leading ladies in Hollywood in the 1940s, along with Katherine Hepburn, Joan Crawford, and Bette Davis. Norman first got to know her when she moved over to William Morris along with Allenberg after the merger, and she immediately commanded his respect. She taught him so much about the business from day one, and her advice was invaluable. After all, she had been working nonstop since she was a small child in silent films like Rudolph Valentino's *The Sheik*, when Hollywood Boulevard was still a dirt road. She knew what it took to get to the top and stay there. Here is one of her gems: "Norman, I know that you represent some young ladies. Always make sure that they handle themselves with dignity and class. Then, they can be in the business as long as they want." When he often repeated that advice, prefaced by the words "Loretta Young told me if you want to be a success . . . ," it was heard loud and clear and taken seriously because everyone respected Loretta.

She told Allenberg, "I'm staying with the Morris office but under one condition. Norman is young enough to be my son, but I like the way he does business." That was one big reason he was sitting in her home with a proposition to present.

Norman told Loretta that if she moved to television, she could set up her own production company like Lucy and Desi. She could be the producer and the star, and they could get her top money to handle all those things, about $5,000 per week. It not only seemed like a good move to her financially, but it made immediate sense in some other, very important ways. At that time in her career, she could still do movies, but maybe not as many as before and only when she felt the roles were right. Television, she recognized, was a powerful communications technology. The anthology show that was on the table would give her a chance to tell the kinds of stories she thought were meaningful. She called it "the opportunity to get one important idea into the mainstream of America

Meeting with Loretta Young and her husband, Tom Lewis

every week." Loretta set up shop at Goldwyn Studios and loved doing the show so much that she often slept overnight in her dressing room during production.

The Loretta Young Show became an instant success. Women especially were captivated by a moment at the beginning of the program that essentially became her trademark. Loretta adored fashion, but during the first few episodes, the show's costume designer was clearly upset. Very little of the original dress creations was visible on the tiny television screen when she came into camera frame to introduce each evening's episode. Loretta came up with the solution, entering the set by opening two tall white doors and turning to close them with an elegant swirl, revealing the contours of her dress with the natural flair of a high-fashion runway model.

When other big names saw what happened when Loretta tested the waters of television, they decided to jump into the pool too. One day, Loretta's publicist called to say that another of her clients wanted to meet with Norman. He took the meeting and soon thereafter made a deal at NBC for another big Hollywood leading lady: Barbara Stanwyck. She had starred in such Hollywood classics as *Double Indemnity*, *Ball of Fire*, *Stella Dallas*, and *The Lady Eve*. From that base, they later put together her deal for the classic Western series *The Big Valley*, which became a huge critical and popular success for her, equal to her celebrated films. TV would keep her in the public eye for the rest of her life.

On a personal note, I had the opportunity to briefly meet Barbara Stanwyck in the early 1960s. I remember it like it was yesterday, but not for the reasons one might think. My father and I stopped at her home in Beverly Hills near Coldwater Canyon Park. He had some papers for her to sign. As they went into the living room, I parked myself on the short stairs adjacent to where they sat on the sofa. For good reason, I can recall what I was wearing that day: a blue blazer jacket and itchy woolen trousers. I also remember vividly how comfortable the white plush woolen carpet that I was sitting on was. When I got up to leave, my gray pants had suddenly turned white. I was covered in lint from the rug. I wasn't bothered by it, more intrigued by the display of the power of static electricity. Memories from childhood are weird animals. I can recall that Miss Stanwyck seemed pleasant enough and was genuinely friendly toward me in those fleeting few minutes, but that carpet made a more lasting impression.

Big stars notwithstanding, since there were so many more jobs to fill, this new medium of television also provided an excellent and greatly expanded platform for new talent. There was one other side benefit that made his job easier. Long before the invention of videotape, a technology called kinescope was used. It was an inexpensive albeit low-quality way to copy a television show by literally pointing a film camera at a monitor. It was essential once the television networks went national. Live programs in New York were filmed in this way and rushed to the lab so that the same program could be recorded and rebroadcast at the corresponding hour in the earlier Central, Mountain, and Pacific time zones. As a result, Norman had reels of material to showcase what their clients were doing—a great tool to build talent and make deals.

Ultimately, the industry's trepidation about television was unfounded, parallel to the fact that Norman wasn't demoted but ended up with an opportunity of a lifetime. And neither did the William Morris television department stay in that beige garage for very long.

In recognition of his pioneering contributions, Norman received the Governors Award from the Academy of Television Arts and Sciences in 2011, the first time an Emmy had ever been awarded to an agent.

Regarding Loretta Young, one of the great gifts my father gave me was the opportunity to work with her, handling her public relations during the last fifteen years of her life. I could easily see why they had a tight friendship for more than half a century. She had an amazingly magnetic personality, a wonderful sense of humor, and was generous in spirit. She lived in the present and did not dwell on the glory of her past, but if she was in the mood to talk about her history, I would be spellbound. She also lived her Catholic faith in both word and deed. Most surprisingly, she was willing to go into the trenches and get dirty to help others, volunteering thousands of hours at hospitals without calling attention to herself. She was also notorious for having a "swear box" on the set of her show. She was quick to point out that fines were only assessed for saying the Lord's name in vain and other religious references, not for the f-word and other common forms of profanity.

Like my father's experience, I too learned a lot from just being around her, soaking it all up like osmosis. Had she not gone into acting, she could have had a stellar career in marketing and branding thanks to her savvy and acumen. She seemed to always be two steps ahead in her thinking, ready and able to handle any situation that might come up.

One such case was a priceless lesson on spin control: how to tell a lie that isn't a lie. Speaking to a journalist from *Interview* magazine in 1987, Loretta spoke about all the leading men she had "crushes" on (including Spencer Tracy and Tyrone Power). She was a sitting duck for the inevitable question about Judy Lewis, her out-of-wedlock child with Clark Gable. Had she admitted it in 1935, her career would have been over in a flash due to the studios' morality clauses in their contracts. Instead she went on a sudden long vacation "to recover from exhaustion" and months later joyously "adopted" a child. Half a century later, she still stuck by her guns, even though such subterfuge was no longer necessary. (Loretta admitted the truth in an authorized biography, which she stipulated would be published after her death, and had told her family that the incident would be considered a "date rape" in modern terms.) But her answer when the question came was perfect, succinct—and a topic killer. With a little chuckle in her voice, she would tell the reporter, "It was a rumor then. It is a rumor now."

One irony of this challenge in the early days of television was that getting big-name actors to move from the big screen to the little one became an opposite problem. For actors who became popular on television, transitioning from TV into movie roles was an almost impossible task and remained that way for a few decades.

Such was the case for a young Clint Eastwood, who Norman had signed to the agency. He had made a name for himself playing the character Rowdy Yates on the popular long-running TV Western series *Rawhide*. Following the example set by Mr. Lastfogel in assigning new clients to him, Norman shared the wealth by attaching a younger agent named Lenny Hirshan to handle the day-to-day for Clint. Hirshan would go on to represent Clint for well over half a century.

Clint wanted to branch out and do films, only to be met unsurprisingly with a stone wall in Hollywood. Carol Levi, an agent with the

Clint Eastwood

office in Rome, came with an offer for Clint. Although Carol was highly respected among her peers, there was hesitation at the home office—no one had heard of the Italian filmmaker attached to the film, and the lack of track record was a major drawback.

Italian cinema in America had an unsavory reputation at the time, with the exception of art house favorites like Federico Fellini and Vittorio De Sica. Rather, it was best known for lavish and over-the-top dramas in togas and other heavily costumed affairs. When the studio system disappeared in the 1950s and actors no longer had their regular paycheck and all the support services supplied by studios like MGM, Warner, and Paramount, many American actors went to Italy to help pay their mortgages. Ricardo Montalban, dropped by MGM, recounted how trying to do anything with a really bad script was the ultimate test of any good actor; *La Cortigiana di Babilonia* (a title that rolled off his tongue like nectar) was the prime example from his résumé that he did solely for the payday.

Understandably, there was neither excitement nor any large measure of support for this project at the agency, but Clint wanted to do it. Because compensation for services by unknown entities was dodgy at best, payment needed to be made in advance, in cash, before talent got onto an airplane. One of the agency's young business affairs attorneys actually met the producer's representative in the William Morris parking lot in Beverly Hills to hand over bundles of banknotes, like they were paying a kidnapping ransom or doing a drug deal.

Some months later, cannisters of the finished film were delivered to the screening room at William Morris. Norman, Lenny, and a number of the other film agents watched the film. Although it was in Italian, it really didn't matter. Everyone agreed that *Fistful of Dollars* was going to be a smash, Sergio Leone was a master, and Clint Eastwood would never have to do television again.

CHAPTER 7

Marilyn and Norman Eat Dinner

THERE WAS SEEMINGLY NOTHING OUT OF THE ORDINARY THE EVENING sometime in late 1951 or early 1952 when Norman escorted Marilyn Monroe into the Brown Derby restaurant at 1628 North Vine Street in Hollywood. Marilyn had just appeared on a television show at NBC studios, just a block away, so a meal at the Brown Derby was a natural choice. It was on the circuit, a popular place to see and be seen, so much so that actors would have their publicists call the restaurant and have them paged to ensure they would be noticed. And it did not take long before Marilyn and Norman were noticed.

Norman thought he could kill two birds with one stone by having his client on *Lights, Camera, Action* earlier that evening, a kind of *American Idol* competition among three primarily unknown or up-and-coming actors. Since it was a respected showcase, Hollywood casting agents were known to avidly tune into the program each week. Not only would this broadcast be good exposure in the industry for the not-yet-famous Marilyn, but Norman also hoped to get a copy of her live appearance in kinescope film to shop around and help get her more work.

He had the duty, almost daily and often nightly, of driving and escorting clients of the office to various appointments, including auditions, meetings with producers, and performances on radio shows, motion picture sound stages, and the new medium of television. It was a part of the job he truly relished. He loved the fact that the guards at the gates of MGM and the network studios in Hollywood knew him by name: "Good afternoon, Mr. Brokaw."

Without question, Norman was there principally to hold their hands, calm nerves, encourage and praise, or console and comfort if outcomes turned out less than satisfactory.

But there was undeniably another agenda for his presence: to make sure that everything went according to plan, to what was mutually agreed beforehand. There was no place for surprises, ambiguity, or miscommunication—a good reason for every scrap of paper generated at the agency having the motto "Put It in Writing" at the bottom of the page. Norman was there as insurance to make sure everyone was professional, and that a vulnerable client would not be exploited in any form. He was happy to be "the bad cop" if required. There was also the matter of scavengers, sweet-talking competitors on the prowl from other agencies who would prey on unaccompanied talent.

Being out with Marilyn was not business as usual, and not for the reason one might assume. After all, she was the protégé and paramour of his powerful uncle Johnny Hyde. Their story has been the subject of films and books. Hyde was at the highest echelon of players, yet he put his personal reputation aside to transform Marilyn from a photo model and starlet into an actress who would be taken seriously. *This Year's Blonde*, title of a TV movie from 1980 detailing their relationship, summed up the shoulder-shrug response from his peers. No stones could be thrown, for each of them had their own peccadilloes. The actor playing Norman in the TV movie admirably captured his eager and winsome personality.

One of Norman's first encounters with Marilyn happened some months earlier at his uncle's home. Coming to drop off a package, Norman was about to sit down on a sofa when he was interrupted mid-squat by a gasp and a scream. He hadn't noticed the object he could have crushed—the plaster model prepared by the plastic surgeon of Marilyn's soon-to-be new chin.

"Marilyn and I hit it off well," Norman recalled. "She knew I was Johnny's nephew, but that didn't enter the picture. What she knew was that I knew where to go with her. Very early on, I remember getting her one of her first jobs at $55 a day, which was Screen Actors Guild scale." He recalled how he felt slightly embarrassed driving her around in an older, less-fashionable car. His quick solution to spruce it up was

Johnny Hyde poolside with Marilyn, *Alamy*

to remove the clunky and antiquated running boards along the sides of the chassis.

Another frozen memory fragment that stuck in Norman's mind was Marilyn's unplanned encounter with his newborn twin sons in early November of 1949. "I used to live on Radford Avenue one block from Republic Studios in the valley. I remember that Marilyn and I stopped by to leave my car in the driveway because it was hard to get a parking space at the studio. I never forget pulling into the driveway; there stood a nurse and my young wife holding our twin sons, getting ready to go for their six-week checkup."

It was an undeniable fact that Johnny Hyde was dying and wouldn't make it through the next year. His obsession with Marilyn was a double-edged sword, perhaps extending his life but maybe also killing him. Heart disease ran through his family, finishing many off in their fifties, with Johnny being the latest victim. The ever-present lit cigarette in his hand didn't help matters.

In the months leading up to their dinner at the Brown Derby, Norman had gladly done the grunt work for his ailing uncle. "Everyone in the office knew that Johnny was not well enough to go with her at night," Norman recalled. "I was the one closest to her, so I had the responsibility for taking her out to interviews and functions. If he couldn't go, I was the one. They knew that I was the young fellow who's involved and always complimentary how I handled her."

Despite his deteriorating health, Johnny worked on convincing his studio head colleagues to take a chance on Marilyn. There was pushback. As much as they wanted to do a favor for Johnny, almost everyone passed, not viewing her as anything special. One month before he died, he finally succeeded in getting her a contract with 20th Century Fox.

Room 517. That was the room number at Cedars of Lebanon Hospital on Fountain Avenue in Hollywood burned into Norman's memory. He drove Marilyn there for what would be the last time they would both see Johnny Hyde. He died on December 18, 1950. Two and a half years later, I would enter the world in the maternity ward of the same building, which was later repurposed as office space for the Church of Scientology.

Not long after Marilyn and Norman sat themselves down at their table at the Brown Derby, Bill Frawley walked over to say hello. A character actor from the movies, he was now starring as neighbor Fred Mertz on the enormously popular TV comedy series *I Love Lucy*.

"This is a young lady we believe in named Marilyn Monroe," Norman said as he introduced her. It did not take long for Bill to cut to the chase.

"I wanted to let you know that I'm having dinner now with Joe Di," Bill said in a quieter voice to discourage eavesdropping. "He would like to meet the young lady. When we're through, we'll drop by your table."

When he left, Marilyn looked at Norman and asked, "Who's Joe Di?"

"He's Joe DiMaggio. He was one of the greatest baseball players of all time, like. . . ." Norman rattled off some of the other big names like Babe Ruth, Lou Gehrig, Jimmie Foxx, and Hank Greenberg, not sure whether Marilyn knew them either. DiMaggio had just retired from the game.

Norman paused for a beat and then warned her, "When I introduce you, I can tell you that he's going to call for your number."

Finishing their dinner first, Norman and Marilyn stopped at their table. The introduction was made. The rest is history. The couple dated for about a year and a half before getting hitched.

Many months later, Norman got a call from Joe DiMaggio. He was having marital problems. He said it was important and asked to see Norman right away. Norman was fresh off the plane from Europe and was watching his five-year-old twin sons. Unshaven, he got into the car and drove to the Beverly Hills Hotel. He found someone to watch Sandy and David and went behind closed doors with Joe.

Marilyn was no longer a client at the time. Johnny had been dead for a couple of years, and no one in the agency except Norman had shown much interest in her. It is entirely fair to speculate that Norman may have not actively pursued representation to avoid any appearance of riding the coattails of his uncle. The appearance of nepotism can be a lose-lose proposition. If he became successful, people would dismiss it as all due to the unfair advantage of his late uncle's influence. If a failure, they would scornfully say he didn't measure up. Nevertheless, an important studio contract had been misplaced due to a clerical error. It was the last straw, and she moved to another agency. So Norman came to see Joe as a friend with no ax to grind.

Marilyn was just starting to do some major film work, and Joe was very upset about it. He may have been a legendary sports hero and hugely popular public figure, but he guarded his privacy intensely. Yet he was married to one of that era's hottest and most heavily publicized star. It was creating what seemed to be an irreconcilable source of conflict. She was about to go off on a USO trip to Korea to perform for the troops, and it was bothering him tremendously.

Norman's advice to Joe cemented a wonderful lifelong friendship. For years to come and up to a few months before Joe's death, the two would meet regularly for dinner whenever Norman came to New York or Joe was out in California. He told him the following: "I can't think of any actress that I know who would give up the opportunity for a role with a top leading man like Spencer Tracy or Clark Gable." Making reference to Joe's most-hallowed accomplishment on the baseball field, he added, "And I don't know of an actress who could get you to give up the opportunity to go up to bat to try to hit in your fifty-seventh consecutive game."

Their divorce was inevitable. But Joe credited that moment Norman and he had together for helping keep their marriage alive for a short time longer and, ultimately, for preserving his enduring love for her. That love was expressed so eloquently and poignantly by the roses delivered to her gravesite twice weekly for almost twenty years.

Norman and twins David and Sandy visit Joe DiMaggio at the Beverly Hills Hotel (taken a couple of years later, at another meeting)

As an editorial note, it is fair to be a little disappointed that I don't have tons of other stories to tell about Marilyn and Norman, with all the fascination her life continues to generate. Although he loved to regale clients and colleagues with stories about old Hollywood, in private Norman was very protective about talking about his clients, including with his family, a complaint my siblings also echo. God forbid you should ask him anything negative about a client. He would abruptly change the subject.

However, the connection to Marilyn did enter my consciousness in a quite bizarre, head-scratching manner. In fact, I consider it high up on my list of wackiest childhood experiences. Sometime in 1962, my mother, Florence, had another long stay at a mental hospital. I remember the place was not as bad as it might sound, at least in outward appearances: lovely Spanish bungalows, beautiful courtyards, and well-tended lawns that looked more like those of a luxury hotel. The same cannot be said about the kinds of therapies and treatments Florence was probably exposed to within those walls, including shock therapy.

At this time, a late model Dodge Dart pulled into our driveway and out walked a woman who would be taking care of us. She was short-haired, on the far end of middle age, bespeckled, and had a leprechaun-like look consistent with her Celtic roots. She was friendly enough, but my nine-year-old sensibility felt there was something slightly off. She did nothing out of the ordinary that raised any red flags. But there was so much ice flowing through her veins that it made me feel like I needed a sweater. Additionally, she had a strange odor, not from bad hygiene but from an herbal lotion she applied to her thinning scalp. She was really into gardening and composting, and I liked that about her. But it was clear that the gig was wearing her out, having to chauffeur my brothers and I to countless baseball games, God forbid they went into extra innings. She got progressively crankier and more short-tempered. Mercifully, Florence returned to home just in time; the Dodge Dart drove off, never to be seen again.

Part of the problem might have been that our temporary caretaker's last job had not ended so well. In fact, she suddenly needed another gig, and ours happened to the one; it was fortuitous that she was available on such short notice. Only weeks before, this person with the stinky hair had walked into the bedroom on 5th Helena Drive in Brentwood to discover the lifeless body of her patient, Marilyn Monroe. From that moment on, Mrs. Murray became a kind of a stock character in an Agatha Christie mystery. What truth was she hiding? Was she covering for the Kennedys? Was she a conspirator? Did she do it?

It is highly conceivable that Florence was under the care of the same psychiatrist (Ralph Greenson) as Marilyn, so that's how Mrs. Murray ended up with us, since he often placed her as a quasi-housekeeper/nurse to his patients. Not much thought was given at the time to the trauma energy that Mrs. Murray carried into our home, adding to the aggregate of the mental burden my brothers and I carried, later described as PTSD. She was highly recommended, after all.

CHAPTER 8

Kim Novak's Big Brother

IF ONE DIDN'T KNOW BETTER, IT WOULD BE EASY TO READ INTO THE photograph hanging on the wall of Norman's office that this was a couple in love. There is genuine affection on display between these two glamorous people. Their chemistry radiates off the photographic paper.

To set the record straight, the love was real between Norman and Kim. But it was a love in the purest sense and certainly not about sex. Carnal relations with a client, even one as beautiful as Kim Novak or Marilyn Monroe, was in his mind an unforgivable betrayal of trust. He also happened to be married and a father to three young children at that point in his life.

A few years before this photo was taken, Kim was filming a motion picture with Frank Sinatra called *Man with the Golden Arm*, which came out in 1955. During the shooting, Sinatra took her aside and told her that he didn't think Columbia Pictures and its boss, Harry Cohn, were paying her enough. "Come on," he told her; "I'm going to take you over to my agent at William Morris, Abe Lastfogel." Two years earlier, Lastfogel had famously secured a part for Sinatra in *From Here to Eternity*. Things had cooled off significantly for the crooner at that stage. He walked away from the film not only with a best supporting role Oscar but also with a resuscitated and revitalized career—as an actor.

Throughout his long career, Abe Lastfogel was a true master at signing new clients, an ability Norman's close colleague and friend Walt Zifkin believed was singularly responsible for building William Morris into a powerhouse. What Kim Novak would soon learn, he also knew

Kim Novak and her "big brother" Norman

how to matchmake a new client with just the right person on his team. He would stay involved with a grandfatherly-like presence so the client would not feel abandoned or passed over. "So I went in and had a meeting with them," Kim recalled, "and at the end, they brought in this little man and introduced him to me. He had these big blue eyes. I just remember thinking that he was small and wondered what part he was going to play in my life."

After wrapping the film with Sinatra, Kim went off on her very first vacation to Europe. There she met and fell in love with "Count" Mario Bandini, owner of Italy's largest tomato cannery as well as a fertilizer factory. Mentions in the press of his title were always put in quotation marks. Bandini was self-admittedly not a real aristocrat. He was an engineer by profession, but "Count" was a moniker that stuck to him.

"It was my very first love affair," she explained. "It was love at first sight, and I had no intention whatsoever of going back to America and back to work. Are you kidding? Not when I had this wonderful love affair going. I was not in the mood to go back. And of course, Harry Cohn [the head of Columbia Pictures] thought, 'Get back here and get to work!' But orders like that just didn't appeal to me, especially taking orders from Harry Cohn.

"And the next thing I knew, I saw that little man with the big blue eyes. 'What is he doing here, interrupting the violins playing, all this romantic music all around?'

"But that little man with the big blue eyes, suddenly he spoke my language. No, I don't mean the English language, but he knew how to talk the way I talked, simple, gentle, kind."

"Shocking, that Harry Cohn, shocking!" Norman exclaimed. "You mean to tell me he started swearing at you? Shocking!"

"Norman spoke to me in a way that I could understand," Kim explained. "'I guess I could go back to America for a little while and work,' I told him. And I did so because he spoke to me in the right way. And I understood it."

What is so intriguing about this incident is how likely it could have all gone south. Norman arrived in Rome with a job to do, like a bounty hunter returning a fugitive to justice. Kim was a rising star and an extremely valuable asset. Reputation was no doubt on the line. Unreliable, badly behaving actors who did not stick to their contractual obligations might soon find themselves selling real estate or seeking other employment in a much less glamorous industry. On the other side was Kim in the throes of passion, in the middle of perhaps the most joyful and exciting experience of her young life. How easy it could have been for her to tell him to go to hell.

Norman reveled in the human element of his business. He was essentially a salesman, but his product was not some inert, fixed commodity. It took a high level of skillfulness to navigate both calm and stormy waters. He had to have a quick mind and think on his feet. He had to be a good listener. He had to have a pragmatic understanding of the psychology and behavior of each of his clients. There were bloated egos galore, an occupational prerequisite for performing artists to muster the confidence and courage to exercise their craft. So many of my fuzzy memories from the 1950s were of hearing him on the phone stroking a client's ego immediately after their program had been broadcast. "You were terrific!"

There's a part of every actor that is childish. Their jobs of playing roles and pretending to be someone else was essentially childlike in nature, and they were rewarded handsomely for it.

For a good portion of my upbringing, I had no real appreciation of what my father did for a living, much less why he excelled in his profession. It all just gave me a weird taste in my mouth. And some of it was mind-boggling. Who were these good-looking people coming over to our swimming pool on the weekends to hang out while Norman worked on his tan? It is logical that the whole pool thing was following in the footsteps of his Uncle Johnny, so impressed was the young teenager from that famous Esther Williams moment.

Some of these frequent poolside visitors were stars of their own television programs, ones my brothers and I watched: Nick Adams was "The Rebel" and Hugh O'Brien was "Wyatt Earp." As early as five-years-old, I was already wary of their intentions. They all had an unpleasant edge, a grasping energy that made me feel uncomfortable and nervous around them. None of them seemed particularly happy. I developed my own bullshit meter, since their calculated friendliness toward me felt about as real as a wooden nickel. Neither could I fathom what the payoff was for my father. Why was he taking time for these unpleasant courtiers instead of playing ball with his kids or maybe giving his wife some attention? I just didn't get it.

Had I been there in Rome as a fly on the wall, I might have better understood the subtle art at play in his work and how the success he was having in this early part of his career was well merited.

"From there on, I realized that he was going to be my caretaker," Kim recalled, explaining that she actually welcomed his protective intrusion into her personal affairs. "He became my brother, my big brother that I never had. He was gentle and kind. And whenever I would get that little romantic urge and get involved in something I shouldn't, he knew how to speak to me. He was always there to keep my mind on the right page."

Kim wanted me to know that Norman's intervention regarding the "Count" in Rome was not the last. Unexpectedly, he showed up at the door of her East Side New York apartment, which was owned by a recent admirer, Prince Aly Khan. Norman apparently had a very distinctive way of knocking on a door, which Kim called his "signature knock." "He would knock so I'd turn toward the sound to turn me around to face in the direction of my Hollywood home. It was a reminder that I needed to get back to work. I was in the apartment with Count Mario Bandini, and he wanted him gone. That next morning the gossip columns read: 'Norman Brokaw will spread Bandini all over Central Park.'" In America the name Bandini was best known for cow manure, and, as mentioned, "Count" Mario happened to own the largest fertilizer company in Italy.

"I found out that an agent needed to know more than how to make a deal. You have to know personalities. He knew how to work with people. He knew how to understand who you were, and how to help you. He knew how to cry with you, laugh with you, love with you. He cared about who you were and what you wanted. And he took the time, the time to respect your wishes and what you wanted in life. And he also made some good deals for me. He made it easy for me to be in Hollywood and put up with a lot of stuff that I didn't necessarily want to."

According to Kim, Norman even stepped up to teach her how to get tipsy in preparation for her role as Jeanne Eagels, the story of a real-life actress who battled heroin addiction and alcoholism. "He took me to the Luau, and we got drunk together," Kim recalled.

The Luau was a very popular tiki-style Polynesian restaurant on Rodeo Drive in Beverly Hills, down the street from the office. It was replete with outrigger canoes hanging from the ceiling, fake waterfalls, and rattan throne-looking chairs galore. "And yes, Norman, my caretaker agent, set a limit of two 'educational' mai tais so I could learn how to feel drunk without falling . . . falling in or out of love with some mysterious stranger!"

I never once saw my father under the influence of alcohol, so the thought of Kim and him chugging down tropical cocktails with little umbrellas was eyebrow-raising. It was a tough job, but somebody had to do it.

"Look at this painting that Kim did," my beaming father repeated to me more than a dozen times over the course of his last few remaining years. It was a portrait of his favorite dog of all, Lily the standard poodle.

Lily was long gone, but somehow the dog felt incredibly present and alive through the pigments and brushstrokes on the canvas. I could see what it was that Kim loved about him. He was still the big brother with the big blue eyes.

CHAPTER 9

The Man They Called "The Colonel"

"Friendship Is Priceless," wrote Colonel Tom Parker on an autographed photograph to his "pal" Norman in 1960. In the millisecond the picture was taken, Norman looked into the camera with a confident smile of satisfaction. He rested his hands comfortably on the back of the chair in front of him, as if there were no other place in the universe he would have rather been. He was in a truly enviable position. The Colonel insisted that all matters relating to Elvis Presley go through Norman and his boss, Abe Lastfogel. This was a true feather in his cap, another confirmation that all the dedication, training, dues-paying, and hard work over his nearly two decades at William Morris had been well spent.

During this frozen moment in time, the Colonel's eyes are closed, a lit cigar in the corner of his mouth resting effortlessly at a perfect right angle to his face. He is holding with pride a plaque given to him by the agency commemorating their enormously successful association. He looks to be an imposing figure not only in size but also in personality.

This was the type of photo that Norman loved and would eagerly display. The Colonel was regarded as a straight talker, a skillful one at that, so the words he wrote to Norman were viewed as high compliment. Again, these photos on display were documentary evidence to both impress potential new clients and reinforce to current ones that they had made the right decision. Important talent wants to be represented by someone of like stature. And for many, you are only as good as the company you keep.

The one and only "Colonel" Tom Parker

First Marilyn, and then Elvis. It would be hard to find two more iconic figures who came to epitomize popular American culture to the entire world. And as fate would have it, Norman kept company with both. Their personas, especially after their tragic deaths, achieved a kind of mythic status. Like Icarus flying too close to the sun and falling to the sea, Elvis and Marilyn were ultimately too fragile to cope with the intense spotlight of fame.

I remember sitting in a periodontist's chair in Denver a few years ago, amused at the coincidence of my two degrees of separation from the subjects of the two kitschy art posters in front of me, Marilyn on the left and Elvis on the right. Were they hanging there in their youthful beauty and allure to distract me from sharp instruments probing my gingival tissues? How many walls of living rooms, bars and restaurants, and office spaces around the world trade on these icons of immortal fame and glamour?

As a key player of the Elvis dream factory, Colonel Parker has been an easy target for biographers and filmmakers, often portrayed as a greedy, power-hungry con artist. Every story needs a bad guy, and poetic license is easy to take when someone is no longer around to defend themselves. Many questions have dogged his legacy decades after his death. Did he flee Holland and become an illegal immigrant because he was a "person of interest" in the mysterious death of a young woman? Why did he go AWOL from the US Army at age nineteen, and why did he end up in a mental hospital? Did this former carnival barker and dogcatcher take unscrupulous advantage of Elvis and his family to enrich himself?

"The Colonel was exceptionally kind, really a sensational person," insists Irv Schechter, an agent who was assigned by the Morris office as a kind of personal assistant to him for several years during the early 1960s. (He was the same one who later fired Zsa Zsa.) We spoke not long after the 2022 *Elvis* motion picture had been out, and Irv registered his profound disappointment at Tom Hanks's portrayal of the Colonel as very negative and inaccurate. "They try to make it controversial, and there is nothing controversial about this man. He was the kindest, most generous person, and one of the strongest dealmakers."

Priscilla Presley told me that she agreed that the Colonel has not been treated fairly. "I saw Colonel Parker the person. He was the kindest, most thoughtful husband, who took such wonderful care of his wife. I never really experienced the tougher business side of him, but he was excellent at that, and that's what Elvis truly appreciated about him."

"The Colonel became like a second father to me," Irv explained. "Basically, what I did was pick him up from where he lived, take him to the studios, run errands, accompany him to recording sessions, wherever he went. I also served as his secretary, typing out all his letters that went out."

And often, Irv would escort the Colonel to the office, where he would meet with Norman and/or Mr. Lastfogel. The door would be shut behind him, and Irv would wait in the anteroom until it was over. Afterward, they would walk back to the apartment the Colonel kept down the street at the Beverly Wilshire Hotel, the same place where Abe and Frances Lastfogel called home.

Irv took me back through the history to make the point that the Colonel had already made his mark and had retired from doing personal management before he met Elvis. He had handled three of the top country-western artists of the 1950s: Hank Williams, Eddie Arnold, and Hank Snow.

His friend Sam Phillips of Sun Records called and told him, "I have an artist here who I think is fabulous. You should listen to him."

"But I'm retired," he replied. Listen he did, and soon after, they met and made a deal. And the rest is history.

It was the time he spent with the carnivals and circuses that gave the Colonel a grassroots appreciation for performers. They liked him, and this was where he began to hone his craft representing artists. In the process, he learned how to fill an auditorium. Once when riding through Las Vegas to the hotel with him, Irv noticed all the Elvis advertising on big billboards and bus benches, as well as spots on local television. "We're always sold out, so why all this advertising," Irv asked him. He answered, "Because I can never afford to take a chance that it won't be."

Another skill that made Colonel Parker's management career take off was his ability to "count the house," perhaps also acquired from his circus days. Box office determined the artist's income, and naturally it was a place where cheating club owners and promoters could get the upper hand on the unsuspecting. This did not happen under his mindful watch.

But it was his acumen for negotiation that set him apart from the competition, according to Irv. He recounted the time when the Colonel told producer Hal Wallis that Elvis's fee for a film would be $1 million. Wallis replied that the highest he could go was $500,000, adding the sweetener that the role was so good that Elvis should win an Oscar for it. The Colonel said, "If he wins an Academy Award, you have my word, I will write you a check for the difference, for the extra $500,000." Wallis agreed; as a result, Elvis became one of the first stars paid $1 million for a single film. It was a good bet, since obviously Elvis did not win.

In the final analysis, Elvis wanted to have meatier acting roles than the films he had done and was still being offered. Priscilla shared that this was only conflict between the Colonel and Elvis: his desire to become a serious actor in the mode of James Dean. The Colonel wanted Elvis to continue to prioritize performing, especially with the highly lucrative residency in Las Vegas. Elvis had the opportunity to star opposite Barbra Streisand in *A Star Is Born*. The Colonel discouraged it, saying that Barbra might minimize him. It was a decision that Elvis regretted.

During his time with Elvis, the Colonel's services were in demand, but he had a steadfast rule. Someone from the Beatles' office called after Brian Epstein died, inquiring if the Colonel wanted to represent them. The Beatles had met the Colonel a couple of years earlier during that legendary late-night get-together at Elvis's Bel Air home on August 27, 1965 (which Irv had coordinated and witnessed firsthand). Regarding the offer, the Colonel told them, "I only represent one client at a time. I'm flattered, but I just won't do it." He also later passed on Sinatra for the very same reason. "He would give help and advice to others, but Elvis was his only focus," added Priscilla.

The big question remained: I wanted to know from Irv why Norman (along with Mr. Lastfogel) was selected as the chosen one. "The Colonel had antennae." What Irv described was a kind of intuition that gave him sound judgment about people based on what his rich life experience had taught him. "I think it was just the directness, the fondness, and the integrity that your father had. There were other agents the Colonel knew—he knew them all—but it was your father he locked into. Whenever there was a meeting, your father was there. The Colonel just felt extremely comfortable around Norman and Mr. Lastfogel."

Irv speculated further that there was a kind of unspoken bond between the three, a kind of shared life experience that aligned them energetically. Although they came from vastly different socioeconomic and cultural backgrounds, each was a self-made man in his own way. They all started from the bottom and worked their way up. Although he still looked very young, Norman was at a higher echelon, already merit-tested for almost twenty years. These were factors the Colonel's antennae could not fail to pick up. "A handshake isn't what it used to be. You don't see any more that people are so vested in the relationship and build that kind of longevity and trust," Irv lamented.

As a child growing up on the immediate periphery of this world, Elvis and the Colonel did not often enter my mind stream. I never had an opportunity to personally meet either of them, unlike many of my father's other clients. I certainly overheard the Colonel's name when my father was on the phone. There seemed to be an air of formality and respect; the mere mention of the name "The Colonel" conjured in my mind some element of command and authority.

In his stereo console cabinet in our living room, Norman had a small collection of Elvis's vinyl records, none of which I ever heard him play for his own pleasure (his personal taste leaned more toward Broadway musicals, Frank Sinatra, and other crooners from the 1950s). Leafing through them, I found one album cover particularly eccentric, showing Elvis wearing a silver metallic-looking suit and striking one of his gravity-defying, gyrating performance poses.

When I was twelve years old and decidedly more tuned into pop music, my father invited me to come along with him to see Elvis perform in Las Vegas. I can't say that I was jumping up and down at the opportunity, but beggars for the breadcrumbs of my father's attention could not be choosers. So I went along for the ride. Elvis was considered yesterday's news and totally unhip by my younger generation. The Beatles, the Beach Boys, the Rolling Stones, and all the wonderful Motown artists ruled the radio airwaves.

I was totally wrong about Elvis. What I experienced was an awesome concert by a consummate artist, and I eagerly went along to a second one not long after. The only disappointment was that I had hoped to see that metallic suit, but it had long been phased out by the first generation of big-collared, sequin-crusted jumpsuits. One unexpected bonus at that first performance was that I got to sit next to the former heavyweight champion of the world, Sonny Liston, dethroned a few years earlier by that other great American icon, Muhammad Ali. Liston was friendly and approachable but never let a smile crack his stone face.

There was no hang out backstage after these concerts. Irv is certain that Norman interacted with Elvis personally (he thinks he may have a photo of Norman among the guests at Elvis and Priscilla's wedding). Priscilla recalled meeting him a few times during her marriage to Elvis, but it was hardly a hangout. But even the Colonel restricted himself to only a handful of dinner meetings with Elvis each year. "Really? Why so seldom," people would ask him. "Well, you know, he's a young man. I'm an old man. And we discuss only business."

In later years, I regret never getting around to asking my father about his dealings with Elvis and the Colonel. Had our interviews in the early 2010s for his memoir continued, we would have surely covered such an important chapter in his life. But his worsening dementia made that impossible.

One time Norman did bring up the subject of Elvis to me was in late 1973. A Swedish businessman named Tom Lidén had contacted him with an offer for Elvis to do a concert tour in Europe. For whatever reason, Elvis had never performed in Europe; some speculated that it might have had something to do with the Colonel's dodgy citizenship status or worse. Norman got the ball rolling, but before it got much further, Lidén called to say that his financial backers had bailed. "If you ever come to Sweden, please let me know; I'd like to make it up to you," Lidén offered apologetically.

I had spent the previous school vacation doing the train and backpacking thing in Europe and had told my father about the great time I had in Scandinavia. When he mentioned Lidén's offer to me in passing, I replied, "Maybe he could find me a summer job in Sweden?" He did, and off I went. Long story short, when people ask my two oldest children how their parents met, they can legitimately name-drop Elvis.

Quite unexpectedly during another interview conducted for this book, I got another classic nugget about Colonel Parker. "I have another Norman story to tell you about our meeting with Colonel Parker," singer Tony Orlando (also a client, who has his own chapter later in this book) volunteered eagerly. From the tone of his voice, I knew it had to be a good one.

Tony gave a blow-by-blow account of the encounter, acting out all the parts like the consummate entertainer he is. "Norman called me one day, and he says, 'Tony, Colonel Parker saw your show last night at the Hilton, and he wants to have lunch with you. Can you meet us?' I got to the meeting, there's the Colonel, and in walks Norman with a big bag of deli sandwiches."

"Tony, the Colonel has an idea for you," Norman started it off after doling out the sandwiches.

"I'd like to manage you," the Colonel cut to the chase. It wasn't the first time they had met, so there was no need for formalities.

"That's a pretty major compliment," Tony replied carefully, sensing there was something else under the surface.

"Have you ever watched 'The 700 Club'?" the Colonel asked, referring to the popular televangelist cable network.

"Yes, I have."

"Have you ever seen the trinkets they sell on 'The 700 Club'?"

"You mean, like the crosses?" Tony recounted in a somewhat less than enthusiastic tone.

"Yeah. But look; I went to see your show in the same building that Elvis worked. And you had them singing 'amen.' 'Michael rode the boat ashore,' and they were standing up on their feet singing out loud. So here's my idea. I think we should start a Church of the Yellow Ribbon. And then we could sell tickets and have a booth with merchandise; we'd make millions!"

"I have great respect for you," Tony responded. "You managed the great Elvis Presley. You struck lightning with him. I can guarantee you that it is never going to strike twice, and if it did, the good Lord is not going to be very happy with this idea. I promise you that."

Tony recalled, "Norman started laughing, and he just kept laughing and laughing. A real belly laugh. That wasn't typical Norman. So the Colonel turns to Norman and said, 'You're supposed to be the agent. Why aren't you pushing this idea?' Still laughing, Norman told the Colonel, 'Because I don't want lightning to strike me either.' And with that, we all walked out."

Years later, Tony ran into Priscilla and told her the story. She told him, "Do you know something, Tony? As awful as the idea was, when it comes to merchandise, the Colonel was a master. He was right. It would have made millions."

CHAPTER 10

Monkey Business

No one could have predicted anything good coming out of a performing ape who went berserk in Mr. Lastfogel's office one day in 1953. But it did, proving the simple fact that our lives can sometimes dramatically change on a dime, sparked by nothing more than a random encounter or a comment made in passing.

Resulting from this bizarre incident was the growth of an enterprise behind anyone's wildest imagination: a production company responsible for some of the most successful and popular television shows of the 1950s and 1960s, and what would become the world's premier charity dedicated to curing children's catastrophic diseases. That's not to say that without the monkey, none of this would have happened, but who's to say for sure.

When an old colleague from vaudeville left a message for him, Abe Lastfogel called him right back. "You should return every phone call, because the one you don't could be a missed opportunity that could cost you a million dollars," he was fond of saying. "Sure, you can come in," he told the man, who was now a talent manager. Mr. Lastfogel represented many of the top names in show business, but this prospective new client was hardly of that caliber. It was a chimpanzee.

The chimp was seated at an upright piano in Mr. Lastfogel's office. "Let's hear the impression," he said. It was promised that the ape sounded like the popular big-nosed entertainer Jimmy Durante. But there would be no music that day. Regrettably, the performer must have gotten stage fright. He suddenly bolted and ran out of Mr. Lastfogel's office, down the hall into the circular-shaped reception area.

The primate quickly exited the building, ran onto the sidewalk on Canon Drive, and climbed up the nearest lamppost in front. There was quite a commotion trying to rein in the feisty performer. It was coincidental that one of the top character actors of the time on radio and film came out of the office and saw the chimp. He was best known for portraying the gangster or the heavy, with memorable roles in such classic films as *It's a Wonderful Life* and *To Have and Have Not.* In his famously thick New York accent, he told Norman, "I didn't know the Morris office had so many different kinds of clients." His name was Sheldon Leonard.

As they were standing there after the chimp was safely coaxed down from atop the streetlight, Norman suddenly got the idea to talk to Sheldon about a new television show the office had just sold for a client named Danny Thomas. It was *Make Room for Daddy* (later called *The Danny Thomas Show*). They were looking for a director who knew about comedic acting. Norman thought Sheldon might be the right person, so he asked him if he wanted to go to Las Vegas and meet Danny where he was performing.

Danny had seen what Lucille Ball and Desi Arnaz had done with *I Love Lucy.* A deal was made for Danny to do the same kind of show. Desi had pioneered the use of three cameras instead of one, which eliminated the need for multiple retakes and made it a more enjoyable experience for both the actors and the live-in studio audiences. It would become standard practice for most situation comedy production. Importantly, Desi and Lucy had also found a novel way to make a television series a highly profitable venture. Accordingly, the agency made it a common practice for stars like Danny to set up their own companies so they could own their own work.

Norman was a young agent and still a little wet behind the ears, but he had a good hunch about Sheldon and went out on a limb. He obviously needed to clear it with Mr. Lastfogel, who was Danny's main agent and mentor. Just to be on the safe side, he ran the idea first by Mrs. Lastfogel, who was like a mother to him. She said, "We'll tell Abe about it tonight at dinner."

"Abe, Norman has somebody he wants to tell you about," Mrs. Lastfogel followed up as promised at their favorite haunt, Hillcrest Country

Club. Mr. Lastfogel quickly approved. Sheldon would work for six weeks at $100 per week to learn everything he could about that setup. After the six-week mark, they could move up the salary, Norman told him. Sheldon became a director and a producer on that show (and had a recurring role as Phil Brokaw, Danny's fictionalized agent). It didn't take long before he became a partner with Danny as co-executive producers of some of the most successful shows in television history in the late 1950s and early 1960s, including *The Dick Van Dyke Show*, *The Andy Griffith Show*, *Gomer Pyle, U.S.M.C.*, and *The Real McCoys*. The two became one of the most sought-after teams around.

"I remember when Normie brought Sheldon Leonard to meet my dad," recalled Marlo Thomas, Danny's daughter and the star of her own hit show in the 1960s, *That Girl*. "Why he thought this guy who played bit-part gangsters and often in B-movies would be a good television producing partner for my dad, I will never know. But Normie knew, and together they packaged a gold mine of shows." Marlo added that this instinct was hardly a fluke, because he did it again a decade later. "And then Normie brought a young Aaron Spelling to my dad, and together they produced *The Mod Squad*." The show premiered in 1968 and ran for five years. It was influential and trendsetting, featuring three diverse "hippie undercover cops" taking on some controversial social issues of its day.

Danny Thomas was truly without peer in terms of a performer who became a powerful titan of the industry. Perhaps Tyler Perry's production company in the late 2010s comes the closest today. But with so few networks and limited options available to viewers long before cable television and streaming, Danny's accomplishment in having so many hugely popular television series on the far narrower airwaves was spectacular.

Back to the main character, it may be noteworthy that this incident with the chimp was not Mr. Lastfogel's first. Not long after Norman joined the company, he witnessed another such performer, one who could supposedly sing the National Anthem. His boss must have had a curiosity about chimpanzees said to have talent. Right on cue, this earlier chimp went up to a microphone that was set up in Mr. Lastfogel's newly decorated office. The chimp stood quietly for a few seconds, Norman recalled, and then let out two loud groans just before emptying its bowels on the beautiful new burgundy carpet. The manager protested as he and the chimp were being escorted out, "He was just clearing his throat! He was just clearing his throat!"

Norman and "Uncle Abe" were regular visitors to the Thomas home on Elm Drive in Beverly Hills, often unannounced, recalled Marlo. They would usually stride into the den and turn on the television because there was some client on a program they had to see. Her mother, Rosie, would whip up some dinner for them. "Uncle Abe would invariably fall asleep sitting on the couch, and after a while Normie would gently wake him up and drive him back to Aunt Frances at their apartment at the Beverly Wilshire Hotel."

From her perspective as a child, Marlo saw this young little guy who followed Uncle Abe around grow up and become a powerful agent. "He loved the business and had such awe of talent. He really had an innocence about him too. I don't think I've ever met any person who rose as high as he had in any field that really retained such innocence."

Years later, as a really struggling young actress, Marlo would drop by the William Morris building. Visiting Norman's office, she couldn't help noticing all the big photos in silver frames of the stars he represented, especially one of his client Natalie Wood with Steve McQueen. The next time she stopped by, she gave him a wallet-sized photo of herself. On the next visit, she noticed that he had put that same photo in a tiny but equally silver frame, dwarfed by the image of Natalie and Steve next to it. "I thought that was hilarious," she recalled. "He did a joke on my joke."

While many of the programs Danny Thomas produced with Sheldon Leonard live on in various media platforms, his greatest legacy of all might be St. Jude Children's Research Hospital. As the legend goes, Danny was a struggling entertainer and went to Mass to pray to St. Jude Thaddeus for intervention. He put $7 into the offering box and asked for help to support his family, vowing that if he became successful, he would build the saint a shrine. Within a week, St. Jude started to deliver. Danny founded the St. Jude enterprise with the mission that "no child should die in the dawn of life."

I could see through my kid eyes that Danny Thomas really loved children. So many I encountered could be lovable and charismatic when the camera was on them and flick the switch to be total assholes in private. Not Danny, at least not to me in my youthful innocence, and never observed at any time in front of my father and me. That is not to say he wasn't without his detractors among older folk. According to some accounts, he could wield a sharp and sometimes vicious tongue to quickly put people in their place.

The one thing I looked forward to every Christmas was the annual party at the house on Elm. The holiday season was otherwise not a warm and fuzzy time in our household. It was already absurdly silly being some highly agnostic Jews with a Christmas tree in the living room. Nor were there that many exciting things under the tree to open on Christmas morning. There wasn't the plethora of toy options back in the pre-plastics era. A new bike or a new baseball glove might be notable exceptions. Otherwise, my father felt like a prisoner during the holidays, with no office to go to and no one to call on the phone. He could be grouchy with us and extra short-tempered with our mother. So, absent any real competition, the Thomases' party was the only great fun to look forward to.

Kids in my world in the 1950s and early 1960s were not given any special treatment or attention. In my family, my brothers and I were thankfully given a lot of rope as long as we didn't make trouble for anyone. But the world was hardly catering to us. It was an interminably long wait to finally become a teenager and get our passport to independence, the driver's license.

My father's clients and colleagues usually gave us a smile and a pat on the head and then dismissed us without further attention. But Danny Thomas made all the children at the party feel like the center of attention and for once on equal footing with the grown-up. And he gave us cool presents like a Timex wristwatch, much cooler than anything under our tree. As kids in his presence and in his home, we felt like we mattered. And the fact that he founded a charity to help sick children on the macro scale was coming from the same source as the genuine affection directed toward us lucky kids.

In subsequent years, as I entered young adulthood, I had a couple of additional opportunities to hang out with him, and the experience differed little from the warmhearted times I had as a child. In the late

Christmas party with Norman, Candy Spelling, Danny Thomas, Frances Lastfogel, and Joel Brokaw clearly admiring the camel

1960s my father and I drove up to his new home up on a hill with an expansive view from downtown Los Angeles to the beaches and its own private chapel. He cooked lunch for us, fried hamburger meat mixed with a few eggs and scrambled all together. Artery clogging aside, it did taste great with a little ketchup.

One last note on that Christmas party was never knowing who on the Hollywood A-list might show up. I remember seeing old stars like the real-life Jimmy Durante and Edward G. Robinson there one year. The best was when Aaron Spelling dressed up in Bedouin gear as one of the Three Wise Men and led a camel down the street and into the Thomases' front yard. Unfortunately, the chimpanzee was never invited.

CHAPTER 11

Behind Closed Doors

FOR ALL THE SUCCESS NORMAN WAS CREATING IN HIS WORK LIFE, HIS private world was a different matter. From all appearances, it had the desirable trappings. He was a handsome man married to the glamorous Florence, who looked like a cross between Elizabeth Taylor and Debbie Reynolds. They had a beautiful home in Studio City in the San Fernando Valley suburbs, just over the hill from his office in Beverly Hills. They had twin boys and a younger one—all just cute enough to complete an idealized picture of the good life in 1950s America.

This illusion was no defense, however, against the destructive power of mental illness. By the time I came along as the third child in 1953, Florence's ability to cope with the stresses of everyday life had diminished greatly. The pattern that plagued her for her remaining years was that she would function adequately for months on end and then, with little warning, fall into the abyss of mania that would lead to lengthy hospitalizations. She was diagnosed with schizophrenia, which in later times would be reclassified as bipolar, although it appears that both diagnoses fit her symptoms well.

Florence's situation was undoubtedly worsened by a host of factors, including general ignorance and insensitivity, compounded by a society that greatly stigmatized mental illness. Add to that the crude treatments of questionable effectiveness, not the least being shock treatment and tranquilizers later discontinued because of highly toxic side effects. What was also tricky was the sense of isolation and helplessness, specifically the absence of any sophisticated intervention from family members that might have prevented her illness from reaching the crisis point. Frankly, there were not many tools in the toolbox to deal with it, and Florence had the unfortunate timing to live before more-effective medicines were available. A popular movie from 1949, *The Snake Pit*, brought some greater awareness of schizophrenia to the greater public but did little to dampen the sensationalized, horror-like phobia surrounding it.

The situation couldn't have been a complete surprise to Norman. During their courtship, a friend had warned him about "the crazy Herdans." Florence's mother had also suffered from debilitating mental

Norman at the beach with Florence on his left and her sister Lillian (Sara Berner) to his right (late 1940s)

illness. Similarly affected was her sister Lillian, well known by the stage name Sara Berner, a character actress and master of dialects. Her most notable role was in Alfred Hitchcock's *Rear Window* as the neighbor hauntingly crying over her dead dog, yelling out to her neighbors, "Which one of you did it, which one of you killed my dog?!! . . . Did you kill him because he liked you?" She was also a regular on Jack Benny's radio and television shows as the meddling phone operator Mabel Flapsaddle. Because of her talent with voices, she was much in demand on radio and had trouble managing the stress of the workload. She self-medicated with alcohol and amphetamines, which led to her decline and early death at fifty-seven years old. Their father, Sam, spoke with a thick Romanian accent. He was an auctioneer by profession, and a good one at that. He was intense and scary to me as a small child. Norman did a good imitation of him, impulsively throwing his arms up like he was about to hit somebody, only to gently stroke his hair back.

Norman either did not see any symptoms or warning signs in the first days of their relationship or wore the blinders of infatuation and denial. But as her life became more complicated by giving birth to and raising twin babies, cracks began to appear. Norman was also gone from morning to often late at night because of his work, which helped things fall through those cracks. Having a third child, notably me, didn't help matters.

As one example of how his absence from the household played out, one summer day Norman came home early from work and got out of his car. Looking over the fence he noticed me (age four at the time) in the deep end of the swimming pool, alone and unattended. Immediately, he jumped into the swimming pool in his fancy suit and tie and shiny Italian shoes to "save" me. He had no idea that I had been taking swim lessons for many weeks and had the full run of the pool. I will never forget the sight of all the money from his pocket hanging on the clothesline to dry, each bill attached with a wooden clothespin.

It is an impossibly hard call to criticize Norman and his response to Florence's condition given the spirit of the times. In many regards, he did the right thing, including getting her the highest quality care available at the time when she became incapacitated. He also stepped up and made sure his children's needs were attended to, with live-in help dedicated to that sole purpose. Men in the 1950s and 1960s like Norman were regarded first and foremost as breadwinners. Middle-class dads were not usually expected to do much parental heavy lifting beyond putting food on the table and providing a roof over their children's heads. Women were usually stay-at-home-moms. For Norman to take a leave of absence and be hands-on with his children while Florence was incapacitated would have been so unthinkable as to be ridiculous.

Ultimately, the severity of Florence's illness could not be allayed by wishful thinking or well-meaning words. Norman knew the utter frustration and futility of trying to reach someone who was unreachable and totally incapable of reason. I will never forget seeing him in tears, realizing his powerlessness on the porch of Lillian's home, where Florence had holed herself up one afternoon. It is also impossible to unremember the sight of my father hastily removing all the large knives from their kitchen

The fam in 1957—Sandy and David top; Florence, Joel, and Norman below

drawers and hiding them in another part of the house. Things were out of control with Florence that day, and ill-tempered Grandpa Sam was coming over to find out what was going on. Fortunately, the incident did not develop into what Norman had feared. It turned out to be just another day in our pleasant-looking war zone.

You don't need a degree in psychology to see some obvious factors on display in Norman's dilemma. In many regards an adult will create a sugarcoated persona for himself, largely shaped by reactive attitudes. Think of it as doing everything in order to not repeat the pain and trauma of one's childhood. Without question, Florence's illness removed any semblance of safe haven in the beautiful-looking family home Norman had created with her.

If anything, it was as if the ghosts of Norman's past had come back with a vengeance. The death of his father, the loss of the family wealth, the trauma of losing his brother in the war, and his mother's delicate health all freshly weighed on his spirit. From his earliest teenage years, there was no time to be playful with so much responsibility and work on his ambitious shoulders. And by the time he was twenty-two—a new father of twin sons and with an increasingly mentally ill wife—those demons were putting their feet up and making themselves right at home.

What could he do to mitigate this out-of-control situation? The answer was simple: Do the opposite. Become a control freak. Norman started crafting a private world that had little tolerance of chaos, and he would become a firm taskmaster to maintain it. There was never the need for spankings when my brothers and I misbehaved. All it took was a stern glance in our direction to reduce us to tears. On the other end of the spectrum, neither was there time for much play or frivolity. Norman was good for about four tosses of a baseball before he would beg off to make an important business call or attend to some other, higher priority. My brothers and I were always hungry for his approval. Showing him our good report cards from school was always a joy. "Do the best you can" was his mantra, and we all appreciated him for that attitude. If we behaved well and kept up appearances, we had it good. We escaped his disapproval and skated along very nicely.

We realized from an early age that there was a sharp contrast between Norman at home and Norman outside the home. I don't think we, as young children, took it personally that he seemed to enjoy life better everywhere other than at home. There was enough tension and arguing between Florence and him during their marriage, so his withdrawal was also a reprieve to us. Many of the impressions we carried from early childhood still felt legitimate based on what we observed in some home movies found decades later in our late Uncle Eddie's basement. Much of the film was taken at holidays and birthdays, and Norman circa 1958 or 1960 did nothing to mask his discontent, impatience, and discomfort.

Money was also a toxic flashpoint. It is safe to say that each of his children dreaded ever asking him to fork over dough for anything considered nonessential. "Do you know how much money I have to make to pay for this?" he would guilt us, assuming we were up on tax brackets and the like. I know it kind of messed up my energy regarding money, reinforcing a childhood belief that we didn't deserve it. I even felt bad asking for money in business, tending to soft-pedal my negotiations and lowball myself. Years later, I came to understand that the origin of my father's behavior was the fear of losing it all like *his* father had. Ensuring financial security for his family through saving and prudent investment was paramount. Never did he own a publicly traded stock. "Municipal tax-free bonds" was another of his mantras.

I don't want to give the wrong impression. There were some fun adventures going back and forth between Norman's two worlds. Almost every Saturday morning we would be transported in something that looked more like a winged beast from ancient folklore than an automobile. The bullet-like bosoms on the chrome front bumper and the glistening fins on its backside, plus the extra-soft suspension, gave this chariot the impression of a soothing, gravity-defying glide. But in truth it was just a shiny black late-1950s Cadillac convertible with the top down, upgraded to the latest model every two years like clockwork.

Norman bundled the three of us into the back seat of the massive car and took the wheel. It must have been an impressive sight to onlookers—the spectacle of this winsome, immaculately dressed but diminutive driver with Brylcreemed black hair and sporting a perfect bronze tan.

Behind him were twin boys in matching outfits who sat on either side as bookends to me, their curly-haired little brother.

The trip rarely deviated from the set routine. Like life itself, it was a mixed bag of pleasant parts, tolerated parts, and varying degrees of suffering. The worst of the suffering was the first part of the journey over a windy hairpin canyon road. Not the greatest driver to begin with, Norman gave no extra thought to taking the curves a little more carefully. I could not wait until a welcome landmark a few miles up the road signaled that I had made it again without barfing on my brothers. Our reward was a stop at the Beverly Hills Hotel coffee shop counter for breakfast. As we walked back along the long hallway toward the parked car, he always stopped in a doorway to get a box of his freshly laundered shirts. A few minutes later, we would arrive at his office, where he would pick up his mail from a slot in the mailroom and quickly peruse it at his desk, neatly tearing into small pieces any correspondence not worth keeping.

Entering the world of his office, even on a quieter Saturday morning, we could see for ourselves why he loved it there and preferred it to being at home. That's not to say that lunacy didn't happen at his work; it did frequently. But from those less-convoluted situations, you could more easily turn the page.

The Morris office was immaculate and had that 1950s modern symmetry, uniformity, and flow that oozed order, command, and power. Walking down the long first-floor hallway was like running the gauntlet, passing all the outer stations and trying not to get detoured into boring side conversations like "My, have you grown" (unless we were being bribed with chewing gum from a desk drawer). We reveled at coming into this inner sanctum and knew on a primitive level at the time that important stuff happened within its walls. The look and smell of all the office machines fired up our imagination—the typewriters, Dictaphones, Rolodexes, filing cabinets, and desks filled with pads, paper, and boxes of erasers and brand-new unsharpened pencils. There was nothing not to like.

Before heading back home over the same canyon, we would walk down the street for one last stop at the nearby Beverly Wilshire Hotel, where the Lastfogels lived. This was more of a mixed bag. It was akin to a military inspection as we were paraded and expected to be well behaved and hopefully cute, like poodles fresh from the grooming salon. We found Mr. Lastfogel, who was even shorter than Norman, to be a quiet, smiling, warmhearted man who really didn't say much to us. Mrs. Lastfogel, former vaudeville performer Frances Arms, did most of the talking. I was afraid of her, knowing that anything goofy I said could evoke a benevolent tongue-thrashing from her. As the audience was nearing its end, she would open her handbag and give each of us a silver dollar. It felt so heavy and big in our small hands. Back then, a dollar was worth more and went a long way.

In my rebellious youth, I looked back on these early years quite harshly. I felt deprived because my father was so emotionally unavailable, although I never felt abandoned and always sensed his protective spirit. Unanimously, we felt that he was the ultimate greatest dad when we were in dire straits and needed rescuing. But there was a sense of loneliness in never really receiving the generosity of his attention or the smaller touches, an unsolicited nod, a wink, or a pat on the back when I might have needed it. That felt like pulling teeth. It was easy for us to think we were just like the photos in his office in the silver frames, a part of the display. As maturity and wisdom is cultivated with age, one learns not to see the world in such black and white but more in gradations of gray. Failures and shortcomings diminish in importance, and gratitude and appreciation often accumulate in their place.

One remarkable moment rises above all to epitomize what it was like having Norman as our dad. We had a problem one afternoon in 1961 when my brothers and I wanted to play baseball in the driveway. Florence's station wagon was smack in the middle and had to be moved, and she was nowhere to be found. David, the older twin by thirteen minutes, found her keys, sat himself behind the wheel, straining to peer over the dashboard, and turned on the ignition. Sandy, the younger twin, started laughing hysterically at how ridiculous David looked. The car lurched forward in short jumps as David reached down to the gas pedal and got the feel. A few seconds later, the neighborhood filled with the sound of shattering wood and crushed metal. David had miscalculated and taken out the side of the carport and done an equally impressive job on the car. Our neighbor rushed over, veins popping out of his bald head, and read David the riot act. If he was that upset, we feared what our father's temper would be like. For the next four hours, we were like prisoners awaiting execution. At the appointed time, Norman arrived, and we must have been a pitiful sight, trembling in our sneakers. He took one look at all the damage and kind of shrugged his shoulders, perhaps with a sense of déjà vu, remembering all the small calamities he had caused as a boy. "We'll take care of all of this."

CHAPTER 12

Exclamation Points!

OF ALL HIS CLIENT RELATIONSHIPS IN THE EARLY 1960S, NONE appeared to be as close as the one Norman had with Natalie Wood. Or at least that is how I perceived it as a young kid. Although I only met her once in person, her energy and presence felt infectiously near. Natalie was a major A-list movie star in the early 1960s. And it was no accident—she was the complete package. She had that rare appeal that attracted admirers of all ages and genders.

I was excited to speak with Robert Wagner (RJ), ninety-three years old at the time of our interview, to fill in some of the details. He was married to Natalie during this period (the first of his two separate marriages to her). RJ had a lengthy résumé in film, starting in the early 1950s, and would go on to even greater success in television in popular dramatic series like *Hart to Hart* in the early 1980s.

"We were all so young, and we had so much fun together," RJ said. "Norman was so wonderful to Natalie and myself." He recalled many Sunday-night dinners with Norman, together with Abe and Frances Lastfogel. He shared fond memories as well of Florence, the first I had heard of my mother's inclusion in the social circle of Norman's work life. That could explain why I felt the relationship was closer than with my father's other clients. Knowing Florence, she must have talked frequently about them, enough to make me feel that they were a kind of extended family. In fact, we also had a quasi-family member living with us—a talking mynah bird that Natalie's mother, Maria Gurdin, had rehomed with us. The bird would always chirp out "hello" whenever our telephone rang; most impressively, he imitated the neighing of the neighboring horse, whose stall was just on the other side of the fence.

One of the photos in Norman's office was a stunning picture of Natalie. She inscribed it to him heartfully: "You have done so much for me—how can I ever thank you? You're the best! Fantastic! All my love, Natalie." The exclamation marks were most definitely not out of character for her. Given his propensity for superlatives, it is safe to assume that the magnitude of her enthusiasm had found its match in a true kindred spirit like Norman.

"All those great films like *Splendor in the Grass* and *West Side Story* Natalie did during our marriage were deals that Norman did," RJ recalled. "He did such an incredible job for her."

My one encounter with Natalie and RJ around 1960 is one of my most cherished memories from childhood, one I can roll back in vivid Technicolor. They took my brothers and me to the Ringling Brothers circus. It was a very simple but genuine act of kindness and generosity on their part. But the whole event took on a kind of spiritual dimension for me. Natalie took such delight in watching our enjoyment. The spectacle taking place within the three rings was magical enough, but her loving energy as she watched over us supercharged the experience with an intensity that is still hard to explain.

As we continued to talk, it became clear that I wasn't going to emerge with a wealth of stories about their time together. But something more important revealed itself. RJ's voice and clarity of thought at age ninety-three was astounding, as if the passage of time had not diminished him since our encounter more than sixty years prior. Rather than telling me stories of who did what and when, he was conveying something much deeper. I realized that revisiting this chapter of his life was emotionally poignant for him, looking back on his youth with the wisdom of old age. Perhaps he hadn't paused to reflect on this special time with Norman and their friendship for many years. Just when I thought this wonderful conversation would leave me with little content, he said this:

"When Natalie and I broke up, it was devastating. But he was there for both of us."

86

Natalie Wood

Norman with Robert Wagner at the Trevi Fountain in Rome

Both of us? My natural assumption was that Norman would have been forced to choose sides. Anyone who has gone through the pain of divorce experiences the parting of the seas as friends and associates realign. Naturally, he would have been expected to choose Natalie, and for good reason. She was the hottest box office attraction of that time. If a studio wanted a dark-haired actress for a leading role in a major motion picture, Natalie was their first choice. I couldn't hide from RJ my amazement at how Norman could have navigated this.

"He cared about both of us," RJ answered with a passion that made the hairs on my neck stand up. "In fact, Norman has always been there for me during the hardest times of my life. He was there for me when Natalie died, and his support and love were just incredible."

I have made many discoveries about my father, both monumental and minute, during the writing of this book. It did not sound that way at first blush, but RJ's powerful revelation about Norman "being there for both of us" became hauntingly penetrating the more I thought about it. It still gives me chills.

CHAPTER 13

Hillcrest

FROM MY EARLIEST RECOLLECTIONS, I WAS CONVINCED THAT NORMAN had next to zero social life outside of his office, or so I thought. The only exceptions I noticed were the occasional dinner or Sunday-afternoon pool party with immediate family like his brothers, cousins, in-laws, or, rarer still, an old family friend from the old days in New York. Wouldn't it have been healthier for him to have some normal friends from other walks of life than show business? Everything revolved around the business, and I admit that I viewed this rather negatively. It felt stressful and not at all fun from my perch on the periphery. Most of those I met failed to make me see any significant charm in them. They all seemed to have a kind of grasping energy, currying favor to advance their personal agendas. They all seemed so miserable and made me conclude from early on that there had to be something better in life than this.

The truth was, I was only seeing this from the window of a very tangential slice of his life. I hate to admit it, but it has only been thanks to the process of putting this book together that I have been able to better understand and appreciate that part of his life (and be therefore less judgmental). Long story short, what I thought was a social deficiency in a workaholic was really a man who was having a great time. He had absolutely no need to venture outside of that circle.

In fact, most of the hobnobbing he needed to do was conveniently concentrated in one place—one-stop shopping, so to speak. Hillcrest Country Club, a ten-minute ride from the office, had it all, the best of the best rooms for Norman to work. If Hollywood royalty of Jewish descent needed a palace to call home, Hillcrest was it in spades. It was born out of necessity, since all the other like places in Los Angeles in the 1930s and 1940s were "restricted," meaning no Jews could be members. Jack Benny; Milton Berle; Harpo, Chico, and Groucho Marx; George Jessel; Eddie Cantor; Danny Kaye; and George Burns all liked to play golf but had no place to go. Groucho had to make an exception in his rule: "I would never be a member of a club which would have me as one of its members." Early members included motion picture studio pioneers Jack Warner, Samuel Goldwyn, Adolph Zukor, and Louis B. Mayer. Every detail at Hillcrest—its world-class golf course, tennis courts, swimming pool, spacious gathering places, wonderful cuisine, and gracious staff—all projected an understated but tasteful elegance. Its architecture and interior design had a welcoming ambience that made everyone feel at home.

When Hillcrest decided that two wrongs did not make a right and elected to open its membership to Gentiles, Groucho had another classic quip. He was an influential member of the board, and they were deliberating about making Danny Thomas the first non-Jewish member. Danny was there all the time as a guest of his comedian friends who congregated around the famous round table in its informal Grill dining room. According to Marlo Thomas, Groucho said, "Look, I don't mind making a non-Jew a member of the club. But couldn't we at least pick somebody who doesn't look Jewish." Once admitted, Danny made it a habit to bring Marlo and the rest of the family to Hillcrest for Sunday brunch immediately after Mass.

It was extremely difficult to become a member, and it was one of the happiest days in Norman's life when he got in. I used to joke that my father didn't need to reach Nirvana because he had found the real deal at Hillcrest. Applicants had to have donated at least 5 percent of their income to charity over the previous five years and dedicated one hundred hours of time to a nonprofit community organization. This charitable factor created a common bond among the members beyond their business dealings and their golf handicap. Norman had proven his merit in this regard many times over, raising millions for Cedars-Sinai hospital.

One he was "adopted" by Abe and Frances Lastfogel, Norman's frequent presence at Hillcrest was never demanded but understood as mandatory, a welcome price of admission to the coveted inner circle. At their table was where Norman suggested to his boss that Sheldon Leonard join Danny Thomas's television team. Norman was not expected to be there every evening, having been cut some slack because the Lastfogels knew he was married and had young children. His close colleague Sam Weisbord, who was single, had no such excuse and therefore occupied the unofficial slot of adopted son number one. The company's lead attorney, Morris Stoller, was also a regular participant, along with a few others.

Hillcrest became an extension of Norman's office, an escape from formality and an opportunity to break bread (excellently prepared cuisine, I might add) and schmooze in a cozier, neutral setting. He didn't play golf, and tennis was not as effective for social networking, so mealtimes took on that role. Client Mark Spitz (discussed in great detail later) recalled his delight in Norman taking him there: "We would have lunch at Hillcrest once a month, for a long period of time. Always seated at the next table was Adolph Zukor [one of the founders of Paramount Studios],

Working the room at Hillcrest with Mark Spitz and Clint Eastwood

who was over one hundred years old at the time. I was twenty-three years old and felt totally out of place. One time some guy went up to Norm and said, 'Can I join you guys for lunch?' And he said, 'Sure.' Anyway, the guy who joined us for lunch and did it on more than one occasion was Frank Sinatra."

Throughout several decades, Norman held court at a collection of favorite restaurants that were his second choice after Hillcrest, including the Brown Derby, Romanoff's, Jean Leon's La Scala on Little Santa Monica Boulevard, Caffe Roma, Spago—all gone but not forgotten. And he graciously always picked up the check.

People I meet who knew my father often mention how he helped their families during a health crisis. They also will note the pleasure of going out for a meal with him at Hillcrest and elsewhere. I stand corrected. He had everything his heart desired of a social life.

CHAPTER 14

Son of a Gun

NORMAN ONCE COMMENTED ON GETTING A CALL FROM A TOXIC CLIENT: "When you put the phone to your ear, the receiver weighs a thousand pounds." I am not certain, but it is entirely possible he was referencing the comedian Joey Bishop. Norman would rather keep silent than talk poorly about a client, even when it came to some egregiously ill deeds. His most trusted assistant, Mary Feinberg, told me that in the three decades she worked with him, Norman never discussed Bishop. Once she asked, "What was Joey Bishop like?" Norman simply replied, "He was not a very nice person," and left it at that.

Mention the name Joey Bishop today and a broad swath of the American public will draw a resounding blank. But many of those born before 1960 will remember him well. First, Joey Bishop was a bona fide member of the Rat Pack, Frank Sinatra's famous ensemble of entertainers who were the toast of Las Vegas in the early 1960s and the stars of a successful series of motion pictures. The others were Sammy Davis Jr., Peter Lawford, and Dean Martin, and their home base was the Sands Hotel and Casino.

Back in the day, the Sands was the place to be. Las Vegas had not yet become a mega adult amusement park but had a more laid-back feeling, which was mirrored in the loose musical comedy schtick of the Rat Pack. Back then it was a collection of low-rise buildings spread out around swimming pools and a few golf courses. It had all the charm of a motel we might see today off the interstate. Before the end of the 1960s, the Sands started to upgrade and built a multistory tower block. The whole

Joey Bishop

complex was demolished in 1996 to make way for the Venetian, the kind of place that helped transform Las Vegas into a Disneyland for adults.

Bishop himself was a comedian in the tradition of vaudeville, burlesque, nightclubs, and the Borscht Belt. His trademark quip was "son of a gun," and his catalog of one-liners proved invaluable to help keep the Rat Pack show moving and everyone on their toes. As the ensemble faded in popularity after the assassination of President Kennedy (who, through Lawford's marriage to Kennedy's sister Patricia, had been an honorary Rat Packer), Joey had gone on to even greater success thanks to some of the big deals Norman orchestrated.

First came the sitcom in 1961 produced by Danny Thomas in which Joey played a fictional talk show host. The show never really found its groove but hung on until it was canceled in 1965. Two years later, however, Joey got a real late-night talk show, ABC's effort to compete with NBC's king of late-night, Johnny Carson. Despite having great guests and a lively format, it lasted for only two poorly-rated years before they threw in the towel. After that, Joey continued to work but probably resigned himself to a less prominent place in the spotlight.

I may be taking this too personally, but the premiere of the talk show on April 17, 1967, could be viewed a bad omen of what was to come. My father asked if I would be interested in appearing in a skit on the show. I was a very dorky thirteen-year-old at the time, but it paid a fortune at the time: $257 AFTRA union scale. Why not?

The gimmick was that Joey was going to introduce his new production team to the audience. Three chimpanzees came out as his writers. I was to be introduced as his director, with headset and fake horn-rimmed glasses on and a clipboard in my hands. I was given one line: "Thank you, Mr. Bishop; I'm glad to be aboard." At rehearsal, Joey said, "When I squeeze your shoulder, you say your line." No problem. I had about three hours before the *live* nationally broadcast show would start. At the appointed time, I went on stage and hit my mark next to Joey. He squeezed my shoulder. He squeezed it again. All I saw was a fuzzy red light on the top of the camera. I froze so badly I had icicles hanging from my ears. "He's so choked up, he's lost his voice," Joey told the laughing audience. Not only had I embarrassed myself in front of millions of people, I had to face all the kids in my school who got to stay up late to see me bomb. Backstage afterward, Joey's sidekick, Regis Philbin, made me feel a tiny bit better. He couldn't help noticing my visibly miserable state and said, "It was much better the way you did it."

In contrast to Joey, Regis was a mensch and carried an energy of appreciation and gratitude over his lifetime for all the opportunities he'd been granted. And he viewed Norman as a kind of guardian angel. "He had a way of changing your life," Regis explained. "Even if things were not going well, no one [else] could make you feel like you were going to the right place. He made you feel better."

Regis had a successful daytime show on the local airwaves in Los Angeles in the 1980s. When the offer came to take the show to New York and possibly go national, Regis was insecure and asked Norman what he thought. "He said to me, 'If you can hit a home run in Dodger Stadium, you can hit a home run in Yankee Stadium.' I told him that I'd never hit a home run anywhere. But it sure was good to hear. I might not have tried without him being behind me. He was always pushing me, making me feel like I could do anything. He was really the best, the best of them all."

Back to Joey Bishop, it is certainly not fair to generalize, but here goes: Of all the categories of people in the performing arts, I want to guess there are more assholes per capita in the comedian category than any other. Perhaps it is because they are the most naked and vulnerable of all, standing there on a stage with just a microphone, trying to get a laugh and praying not to bomb. Singers are rarely forced to go solo but have fellow musicians, just as actors have fellow actors, to support them. So maybe it's no great mystery that comedians tend to have more insecurities. "Will this be my last gig?" "Will my phone ever ring again?"

In defense of Joey Bishop, it was no accident that he rose to the top of his profession. He was as charismatic as anyone who walks out on a stage. He could be kindhearted and generous and fun. And he was certainly kind to me in my moment of failure.

But from what I can gather, he had volatile mood swings and had a way of picking fights and pissing people off he shouldn't have, Frank Sinatra being at the top of that distinguished list. Apparently, Norman Brokaw too. When I asked George Schlatter about him, he had a one-word description: "Weird." Perhaps it was a brain-chemistry thing; some people feed off the adrenalin and dopamine rush of conjuring drama and conflict. Journalist Michael Seth Starr, author of *Mouse in the*

Rat Pack: The Joey Bishop Story, writes: "I was amazed that Joey was so accessible (he answered his own phone) and that he would take the time to spend hours chatting with me. It wasn't always pleasant; Joey could be sharp, cutting, and abruptly sarcastic. He could get nasty if I didn't laugh at a joke, and if I did laugh, would quiz me as to why I thought it was funny. He could be downright prickly one minute, charming and warm the next. He believed in 'honesty,' he said often, and he didn't hold anything back."

It was not for lack of trying, but try as I have, I have no explanation how or why Joey Bishop stretched Norman's patience beyond the breaking point. There are no witnesses still around to question. I can only speculate:

Sound advice given and repeated but never heeded.

Crisis fatigue, i.e., too many fires to put out and not enough water.

Loss of faith and trust after too many indefensible bouts of nasty behavior.

Fish or cut bait—having to choose sides and do damage control to preserve key relationships that have priority over the dubious needs of a single client.

Slow burnout and gradual withdrawal.

A combination of any number of all the above.

CHAPTER 15

Welcome to the Big Leagues

Leaving the marriage with Florence in 1962, Norman's life became a more delicate balancing act. He was still in his midthirties, and work life was demanding but solidly on an upward trajectory. He was also the father of three children, who were left under the supervision of a highly mentally unstable mother. Some relief on that front was achieved with hiring Mrs. Murray and a couple of other live-in aides. One of them was a likable but stern African American woman. One day, I did something that made her angry with me, and she said something to the effect that she was going to "crucify" me. I didn't know what that word meant and asked my father about it. The next thing I knew, this person was gone.

To his credit, Norman made sure his children always felt the presence of his protective eye, at least when it came to material needs and the more dramatic "shit hit the fan" life situations. As his clients learned, he was someone you wanted in your corner in a crisis; he was the same with his children, both then and in the future.

Norman was also a desirable bachelor. At one point he was seriously dating a religious young woman named Jenny. He must have really liked her, because he had a catechism book at his home. I cannot imagine that someone so uninterested in organized faith would have considered conversion for any purpose other than to please this lover. But he never went through with it. Who knows whether the relationship came to an end over this issue or something else.

"Meet me on Sunday at 11:00 a.m. at Greenblatt's Delicatessen," Norman instructed my brothers and me. "I have someone special for you to meet." The three of us could infer from the formality of it all that this was the ritual "meet your new mom" kind of meeting, where excitement and trepidation cancel each other out to create a "whatever" indifference. It was 1965, and we were two teenagers plus one soon-to-be. We really were not in the market for a new mom or stepmother. We had enough on our hands dealing with our real one.

Mrs. Murray in her Dodge Dart dropped us off across the street in front of Schwab's Pharmacy on the Sunset Strip. By the time we were crossing the street, we could see Suzane Weintraub in front of Greenblatt's with Norman. Introductions were made. I think our first impression of Norman's choice was unanimous. The speech balloons above our heads would all have had a huge question mark. We didn't quite get it; she just didn't seem to be his type.

Sue was born in 1943 in Jamaica, Long Island, and of Romanian Jewish heritage. She was attractive—blonde, pale, and petite. She had been a secretary for Lee Salomon, an agent in the William Morris New York office, and Norman had met her during one of his trips East.

After the brief how-do-you-do's, Norman bought us some delicious sandwiches to go, and we took them with us on a bus that brought us to Dodger Stadium. As we got to know Sue better, we all took a liking to her. What she might have lacked in sophistication and education, she made up for with a New York streetwise perkiness that bordered on mischievousness. Since we were all in various stages of teenage revolt, this was very endearing to us. Being only six years older than David and Sandy and ten years older than I, she took on more of a role of an involuntary older sister.

According to my brother Sandy's recollection, soon after Sue had arrived, she almost did not make the cut. Joe Rivkin, a balding and much older chain-smoker who had a small office upstairs at William Morris, had befriended Sue. We will never know the backstory or at whose urging it came about, but Joe staged an intervention. It was unclear to anyone still alive who remembered him exactly what he did at the agency. In his younger days, in the 1930s, he had been a casting agent, the *Our Gang* comedies among his list of credits. All I knew was that he served as a kind of a fixer, so that may explain part of his part in this scheme. He did favors and errands for the higher-ups. If one of his colleagues needed to get off jury duty, have a parking ticket excused, or arrange free passes to Disneyland, Joe could do it. He was connected. I marveled at his method of smoking cigarettes, especially how the exhaust from his nostrils looked almost jet-propelled. He also made the best homemade pickles I have ever tasted, his mother's secret recipe.

"Joe had a talk with her," Sandy told me. "I can't believe he did this, but he told her, 'You're out of your element here. You need to go back to New York. This is the big leagues here.' He gave her a plane ticket and everything. The next thing I knew, she was still here. I'm surprised that Norman ever spoke to Joe again after that, but he did." However, we don't know who the co-conspirators may have been. In fact, Joe came to the house often on weekends for several years after—more than once standing in the kitchen, thinly slicing cucumbers to make his famous pickles.

I ended up with a good front-row seat to this early relationship. I had moved in with them, telling my father that I could no longer live with Florence, who was having another of her horrible episodes. He graciously consented. They lived in a home off Benedict Canyon up a steep hill. A short time later, David and Sandy also moved in for a short time until Florence recovered and was released from her hospitalization. To everyone's credit, the living situation worked well. Being forced to deal with stepchildren is not any new bride's desire, but it gave the gainfully unemployed Sue a level of meaningful activity. To my delight, she gave me illegal driving lessons in her Mustang in the William Morris parking lot on late weekend afternoons, which she always laughed about whenever we met years after.

That is not to say there weren't initial bumps in the road and other omens that bode poorly for the future. Sue had to realize quickly that it was Norman's way or the highway in most if not all matters. For example, he was a clean freak when it came to the home, and she was anything but in the beginning. She also went to great lengths to ineffectively disguise her smoking habit, spraying air freshener and popping mints. Norman had to know, but he let it go. And being as well off financially as he was, he kept Sue on a very short leash when it came to spending money.

Sunday dinner by the pool with Sandy, Sue, Joel, Norman, and David

However, by tacit agreement, cash and coins left in his pockets became finders-keepers and augmented the budget.

One bonus my brothers and I really enjoyed from being part of Sue's life was hanging out with her family when they came to visit from New York. They were super friendly, interesting, and authentic, dyed-in-the-wool Jews and gave us ethnically deprived kids a wonderful dose of that culture.

Like Joe Rivkin, other people might drop by the house on weekends during this period whose presence in Norman's life seemed improbable if not downright mysterious. Of all the visitors, the strangest of all was a barefoot, bearded, long-haired, nature-loving proto-hippie known as Gypsy Boots. He came over regularly, perhaps once a month over the span of a couple of years, with a big box of fresh produce and nut/fruit/seed bars that were not that appetizing. It would be hard to imagine a more polar-opposite figure to my immaculately groomed and dressed father.

Robert Bootzin (his real name) was always enthusiastic, almost too intense, speaking of the virtues of healthy natural living well ahead of his time. Despite their differences, Norman loved talented people, and it was clear that this lively and charismatic person had loads of it. Gypsy Boot's self-confident intensity and strong conviction scared me a little, but I too was fascinated by him. And I was more strongly influenced than I could have imagined. I must have decided that it was important information to be filed away for future reference. If you're curious, do a search on Gypsy Boots. He was one of the vagabond "Nature Boys" who inspired the legendary song of the same name (written by his buddy Eben Ahbez) and sung by Nat King Cole. The profits from that song alone in the late 1940s built Capitol Records into a powerhouse. Something called a "smoothie" did not exist until Bootzin coined it. His influence in promoting healthy food and natural living was groundbreaking. He was ahead of his time, that's for sure.

From my observation post, Norman and Sue's relationship was humming along. None of the tension from his time with Florence was perceptible, much to my relief. In a humorous way, they had that trophy-wife and trophy-husband thing going on. Norman had a young and lively companion on his arm at restaurants and social events, and Sue had bagged a rich and not-too-long-in-the-tooth husband. No return airfare to Jamaica, Long Island, was needed for the time being.

CHAPTER 16

Mailroom Melodrama

MENTION NORMAN'S NAME TO ALUMNI OF THE LEGENDARY WILLIAM Morris mailroom, and you may hear the same story repeated. Theirs is a chorus of astonishment at how a bigshot like Norman would bother to learn their names, offer guidance and encouragement, and sometimes much more.

As the first graduate of the company's West Coast mailroom in the early to mid-1940s, Norman naturally had a soft spot for what would soon be regarded as a rite of passage for aspiring agents or anyone with wider Tinseltown ambitions. But there was something deeper at work. He treated this pool of bottom-dwelling slave labor as talent not so dissimilar from his clients. And history has shown that it was a sound move on his part. Kindness does not cost very much, and it is rarely forgotten, especially when given in times of need. Valuable relationships that lasted over a lifetime began then and there, including with several persons who used the mailroom as a launchpad to greatness. One classic example is David Geffen, who famously fibbed about having a college degree (a prerequisite for employment). While sorting the incoming mail, he intercepted the fact-checking response from the university to delete the "not" from "did not attend" and retyped it on UCLA stationery he had custom printed for that reason. While others had been fired for submitting false résumés, Geffen had quickly proven too gifted to be dismissed over a technicality, one he confessed to the bosses soon thereafter. Geffen and Norman developed a close association in the decades that followed.

Norman's interest in the trainees was also a simple act of passing along an attribute he adored about the company, the sense of caring family that was always there to help despite all the internal competition, clashing personalities, and the dramas that life served up.

For the mailroom trainees just cutting their teeth, every day was an audition. Activities were usually menial in nature (making a college degree a prerequisite to be hired somewhat silly). Beyond sorting the mail into all the slots and delivering it to specific offices, they would also go out on "the runs," deliveries that might include stops at studios, clients' private homes, banks, and various offices scattered throughout the greater metropolitan area. The more experienced ones might be asked to "sit on a desk"—short for subbing for an agent's assistant, who might be out of the office that day.

So while Norman and other like-intentioned colleagues interacted with these young people, these elders were also assessing them to see if they had the right stuff. Did they have a winning personality and possess the needed people skills? Did they have an eagerness to learn and go the extra mile, treating it more like a marathon than a sprint? Did they appreciate their opportunity and stay focused? Did they rise above mediocrity and show sparks of creativity and intelligence? Did their personal habits and appearance maintain the proper decorum? Did they practice the art of knowing when and how to kiss ass?

Those who performed well on these qualities stood an even chance of becoming "adopted." As soon as an opening was available to become an agent's assistant, the chosen one would ceremoniously exit the mailroom like a young rookie getting their first shot at the big leagues. At the time it may have felt like a huge advancement in the pecking order, but reality would quickly bring the newly promoted back down to earth. Working one-on-one with an agent invited a more intense level of scrutiny.

If not "adopted" within a reasonable time, mailroom grunts would wither on the vine, finally realizing their dead-end situation and moving on to other (and hopefully better-paying) opportunities. I would hazard a guess that perhaps no more than one in four trainees stuck it out with the company longer than eighteen months, which seemed to be the often-heard expiration date. As far as I know, rarely would one of them ever get fired unless they committed some egregious act.

Some flameouts were more spectacular and memorable in nature. There are only so many open slots at the top of the pyramid, and the vast majority of those seeking fame and fortune in Hollywood find disappointment instead. The mailroom was not immune. The "what-ever-happened-to" answer usually meant moving on to some form of Plan B. For others, the consequences of failure took more self-destructive forms, especially when cocaine and other recreational drugs became the popular substance abuse of choice during the late 1960s and onward.

As luck would have it, I was able to dip my toes into this world thanks to a summer internship program for the privileged offspring of the company's upper management. It was my first true introduction to the adult world, as I was still a barely pubescent high schooler, but a few of the fully fledged mailroom guys decided to take me under their wing. With all certainty, their attention wasn't intended to curry favor with my father. Instead, I can only guess they saw a flicker of their rebellious selves in me and treated it as a form of sport by introducing me to the 1969–1970 version of the wild and crazy life. The adventures I had during those two summers could make for an entertaining coming-of-age novella on its own. Not surprisingly, none of my three "mentors" got "adopted" but went on to satisfying and rewarding careers elsewhere.

Despite my immaturity and inexperience, I was aware enough to gather what this game called the mailroom was all about. On many levels, it was time well spent, and what I learned there gave me a solid reference point as I grew older and wiser about the ways of the world. Some knew how to play the game well and persevered to go the distance and become company men. More likely, the bulk had the attitude of come what may. The job sufficed to get their feet wet, make some contacts, and cast a wider net. If it worked out at the Morris office, fine; if it didn't, not the end of the world. And some had other agendas that were far less obvious.

In the latter category was a clean-cut young man I got to know briefly during my summertime stint. He went about his business and seemed pleasant enough. So it came as a big shock to hear some months

Mailroom alumni Norman and David Geffen

later that he had supplemented his $90-a-week salary by also running a stolen and forged credit card ring.

One of my three mailroom mentors (and a lifelong dear friend), Alan Schwartz, discovered this debacle in the most unpleasant way. He reported to work like any other day. Waiting for him were two detectives from the LAPD. They spirited him into a nearby conference room and told him they had a few routine questions to ask.

"Do you know the accused?"

"Of course; I worked next to him."

"Has he ever visited you in your residence?"

"Well, yes. All my mailroom colleagues have. Some more; some less."

More questions followed about their relationship, and then things suddenly became more personal.

"What is the amount you pay in rent?"

"It's a new building, so the rent is high."

"What kind of car do you drive?"

"A two-year-old Cadillac."

"What is your salary?"

"Ninety dollars a week."

Before Alan could say anything, such as "Officer, I can explain," the detectives had heard more than enough.

"Okay, Alan, cut the crap! Why did you do it?"

"Why did I do *what*?"

"You were his accomplice. Admit it now and we'll go easier on you."

Frozen into stunned silence, Alan looked up to suddenly see Norman appearing in the doorway of the conference room.

"Exactly what is going on here," he demanded to know.

One of the detectives, doing his best "just-the-facts" *Dragnet* imitation, explained that they were about to cuff Alan and read him his Miranda rights. "Does a twenty-two-year-old kid making $90 a week live where he lives, drive what he drives, wear the clothes he wears?" Case closed.

"I don't think so," Norman said with authority, suddenly appearing several inches taller than his five-foot-five frame. "Alan, let's call your parents."

"Can't do that," he told him. "They're in Europe." Back then, decades before mobile phones, reaching someone overseas was not an easy task.

Impatiently, one of the detectives motioned to Alan and said, "Come on. We're taking you in. You can clear this up after you're booked."

"You are *not* arresting this boy! He is an employee of the William Morris Agency, and as such I vouch for and take full responsibility for him. *If you arrest him, you will have to arrest me as well. You will not take him from this office!*"

The police backed off but threatened that they would be back. His parents were reached in the immediate aftermath, and they advised him to contact the powerful attorney who had arranged Alan's job interview at the company in the first place. No doubt the cops eventually got the information about the modest trust fund from his late grandfather, which adequately supplemented his income.

CHAPTER 17

Vick Place

IN THE SUMMER OF 1967, NORMAN AND SUE (WITH ME IN TOW) MOVED from one hilltop in Benedict Canyon to another perch a few miles over in the Trousdale Estates area of Beverly Hills. The new home on Vick Place had a dramatic view of the west side of Los Angeles, extending to the western edges of downtown L.A. all the way to Catalina (visible on a rare smog-free day). The area had been developed not long before, and all the planted trees that lined its steep hillside streets were not much bigger than saplings. The homes themselves were a hodgepodge of various modern architectural styles—some impressive, others obvious failures that tried too hard to be clever. Fortunately the new house, while somewhat conventional in its design, fell into the former category.

The immediate neighbors were Ray Kroc, mastermind behind McDonalds, to the west and Thomas Kuchel, former US senator, on the other side. Across the street was actress Terry Moore, who claimed without proof to have been married at one time to Howard Hughes. Around the block lived Gen. Omar Bradley, who served alongside Eisenhower and Patton to defeat the Nazis. Just down the hill was some immediate family to Chiang Kai-shek. Farther away, Danny Thomas had the lot with the best view of all and erected a stately home equipped with a private chapel. Had I been younger, the neighborhood would have made for interesting trick-or-treating on Halloween.

Life in the late 1960s as seen from high up on Vick Place was a mixed bag. Out in the big world, there might have been great pop music, but the Vietnam War, the assassinations of Martin Luther King Jr. and

Bobby Kennedy, and the general spirit of social upheaval gave it a volatile intensity. Inside the home, things were beginning to get a little weird. The carefree Sue I had liked so much was disappearing. She suddenly became this obsessive clean freak, walking around the house with a spray bottle of Windex and a roll of paper towels, wiping down walls, counters, and doorknobs. If anyone needed water from the kitchen sink, she would immediately blot and polish the stainless steel so that no droplets remained from the splash. It would only grow worse with time. As to how this happened, one can only assume that Norman gave her grief about the house not being up to his cleanliness standard, and she developed a textbook case of OCD.

This tension was not difficult for me to be around because I wasn't around much. Joel's liberation day was on July 1, 1969, when I drove my used 1966 white Ford Mustang with a black vinyl top out of the lot of the Santa Monica DMV after passing my driving test. I was a free man with car keys and could see a promised land of college and adulthood just before me on the horizon, with only the last two years of Beverly Hills High School standing in my way. The summer internship program at William Morris also gave me a crash course in the excitement lurking in that brave new adult world.

Another good reason to look for an exit was that baby-making was taking place on Vick Place, first with the birth of Barbara in 1968 and then Wendy in 1969. I had no problem with babies—by that I mean the concept of babies. I just didn't want to hang out with them, a sentiment I'm sure most teenager boys both then and now might share. Barbara was a truly adorable child, given the name of Norman's sister who died in infancy and the middle name of Marie after his mother. Wendy was equally adorable, but we didn't have much time together—I flew the coop to start college.

While there had to have been warning signs before, once Barbara started kindergarten, it was abundantly clear that something was not right. She was hyperactive and started manifesting increasingly difficult behavior. The school psychologist diagnosed ADHD and a learning disability, yet those labels were clearly inadequate given the complexities she was soon presenting. She was clearly high functioning, but her developmental difficulties were sabotaging any potential for growth or inclusion. Her deficiencies in maturity, intellect, judgment, and social skills created ongoing chaos, drama, and turmoil in their wake.

No one can say for sure what may have caused these abnormalities. Heard most was that her brain might have been starved of oxygen during childbirth. Less spoken about was a back-alley abortion in New York Sue had before she had met Norman that could have scarred or damaged her reproductive organs. There also was the procedure to "blow her tubes" to make it easier for her to get pregnant. I remember hearing that some medications Sue was taking might have damaged Barbara's brain, but no one around then besides me can verify that. She was also a closet smoker but had stopped during pregnancy (or so we hope).

Raising a special needs child, especially one with mental challenges, obviously creates enormous stress for a family. If the couple has any loose bolts in their relationship from the outset, chances are parts will soon go flying off. The damage is real, and it takes enormous resiliency and an abundance of caring, patience, and love to work through it all.

Every parent of a disabled child must confront another demon called denial. If the child from all outward appearances looks normal and gives no obvious social clues of being "different," the parent can easily downplay the reality as if it will magically blow over. However, once someone starts looking and behaving "different" in public, the heat intensifies.

When the magnitude of Barbara's issues became irrefutable, Norman stepped up in a huge way, true to his character of being someone you want in your corner in a crisis. Maybe he stepped up too much. As masterful as he was as a problem-solver, he would have a hard time recognizing that he was essentially powerless to do much for Barbara other than provide her with a safe, loving, and supportive environment. But it was not in his character to give up. The one area in which he felt he could do something was her increasing weight. It started to balloon, most likely due to the psych medications she was taking. Appearances mattered to Norman, and Barbara was transforming from an adorable little girl into an obviously abnormal-looking child. Norman became obsessive in trying to get this problem under control, weighing her on a doctor's scale in his bathroom every morning and keeping a tight check on her food intake. It grew into a continuous source of tension—ultimately, fear—in the household, especially when the scale ticked upward. Like what his oldest children had experienced a generation earlier, Barbara and Wendy were intensely afraid of incurring his wrath.

The situation in the home worsened as Barbara's footprint in the community expanded and her interactions grew progressively more complex. Outside of his work, Norman's main priority became Barbara. Her situation sucked up all the oxygen in the family's life. Like many siblings in the same situation, Wendy went along with the program, getting a few leftover breadcrumbs of attention. Holding so few cards of influence, Sue found herself with little clout. Norman ran the show; he was the one with the power, money, influence, and fear. He was still working long hours, and Sue was taking the main brunt of child raising. Barbara grew into Daddy's girl, with Norman staunchly defending her, sometimes to a fault, often enabling and unintentionally making her problems worse. By default, Wendy became branded as her mother's daughter, with complications to follow.

The tension in the home also exasperated Sue's OCD. Wendy recalls how movement of a cookie box, a telltale crumb on the cabinet shelf, or, worse still, a missing cookie or two would not escape inquisition. As the two girls came through the front door after school, she would yell, "Hands up, hands up!" They would be marched directly to wash their hands in the bathtub (instead of messing up a regular handbasin). No finger marks should smear a wall or contaminate a door handle. Food on the dinner table might have an aftertaste of ammonia from an ill-timed Windex spritz. She was also known to take out the vacuum cleaner without warning at inappropriate times. Baseboards in the kitchen would be wiped down like clockwork after dinner with her spray bottle and paper towels. In Wendy's child mind, growing up with this dysfunction was not a big deal. It was so commonplace that it faded into the background, similar to how we can desensitize ourselves to an ever-present bad odor with time.

Wendy was quick to point out in our conversations that her childhood was essentially happy; at its worst were storms to weather that would eventually pass. As terrified as she could be of the stern side of

Norman, she realized even at a tender age how special he was. "I thought he walked on water. I was so proud to be his daughter. When we were out in public, he treated people like gold. You couldn't get out of a restaurant without him talking to everybody. And if I needed to talk to him at the office, he would always take my calls, stopping everything to talk to me on his private line. If I was in trouble in any way, he'd drop everything. He was a fierce protector, and I used to be really afraid of what my life would be without him.

"He was not touchy-feely. He didn't love us in a way where he'd get down on the ground and ask us to tell him all about our day. For example, he wouldn't come to all my tennis matches, but he'd always be there for the finals, holding court, talking to everyone. He would tell me how proud he was of me. I felt it. And I loved it."

Despite growing up in Beverly Hills, Wendy never had the sense that the family was wealthy. "We were comfortable, but I definitely didn't feel rich." She saw how her friends had all sorts of expensive perks from their parents, from toys to cars to apartments. Norman was not so extravagant and kept a tight control on the purse strings, the lone exception being his generosity in always picking up the check for meals out with family and friends. In the long run, the outcome of his preventing his children from feeling spoiled and entitled could be considered more of an enlightened action than his simply being a tightwad.

The real happy place for the family was the two or three times a year they would all camp out at the Kahala Hilton in Hawai'i at spring break, August before the start of school, and sometimes at Christmas. "Dad was in his element there; that's why it was so much fun. Every night we were out to dinner with different people, like Jack Lemmon, Prince Rainier and Princess Grace, Goldie Hawn, John Denver, Michael Landon, and so on. Afterward, everyone would congregate in the lobby, all these entertainment families."

The only blemish on these heavenly trips to Hawai'i was a hide-and-seek game gone terribly bad. Trying to hide from Barbara on the beach, Wendy and a boy named Jonathan got running and didn't stop until they were a mile and a half away in a nearby shopping mall. They were both under five years old, and the police issued an all-points

Impressive suntans at the Kahala Hilton—Wendy, Sue, Barbara, and Norman

bulletin. The governor got involved. When two policemen found them, Wendy was able to give her name and her address on Vick Place. They were taken back to the Kahala, and a concerned crowd was assembled there in the lobby. She saw one of Norman's friends among the group and said, "Please don't tell Daddy." But it was too late. Norman snatched her away and read her the riot act of a lifetime, followed in good measure by a spanking when they got up to the hotel room (one of only two such instances she can recall from her childhood).

A frequent member of the Hawai'i entourage was a middle-aged, heavyset bachelor named Jules. He was hardly a celebrity or a powerbroker. Over several years, Jules was a de facto nanny/gopher, principally for Barbara and often for Wendy to lighten the parenting load. His day job was as a craft services guy, industry lingo for the one who supplies all the munchies and beverages on film sets—a well-liked figure from whom cast and crew could feed on a smorgasbord of snacks to help them make it through the tedious hours on set.

How Jules got adopted into the family sounds a little creepy by contemporary standards. "Every day, my mother used to go jogging at Coldwater Canyon Park and I would go with her. Jules used to hang out there. He and I used to toss a ball while my mom was jogging. And then my mom started talking to him. So he entered our life through me. He used to take us places where we needed to go in his junky car."

"Lean forward," he would command when the groaning car struggled to make it up the steep hill to Vick Place, a naïve belief that shifting their puny combined weight forward was going to make a difference. Despite outward appearances, it was all pretty benign. "He helped us out as a family, so I just accepted it. He was like a friend."

In the long run, the marriage between Norman and Sue could not survive the continually accelerating level of stress. Some may think that the nightmare situation with Barbara was the fatal flaw that single-handedly doomed their relationship. Just as likely, it could have been an integral part of a perfect storm that laid bare the deeper flaws and short-comings each side contributed to the outcome. This mismatch between a powerful husband and an increasingly overwhelmed wife deteriorated into a very ugly divorce.

Those who thought they knew Norman and never heard him utter a cross word had something else coming. Never had they seen him this angry and vindictive. Most unfortunately, the children got swept up in the conflict. "I think that over time, he turned Barbara against our mother," Wendy explained. "Barbara became brainwashed to the extent that she never wanted to see her anymore. I don't think he did it maliciously. I don't think he understood that it would affect her in that way, but that's what happened."

For her part, Wendy got grief if she said anything to him that was protective of her mother. "My mom was so weak, I would say it was my personality to protect her, so I had to stand up for her." Fortunately, his animosity toward Wendy lessened with time.

CHAPTER 18

Secrets

WHEN NORMAN SPOKE OF ALL THE ACCOMPLISHED LEAD ACTRESSES HE had worked with, he always included Susan Hayward near the top of the list. Her Oscar-winning performance as the condemned prisoner Barbara Graham in the 1958 film *I Want to Live* became the benchmark in American cinema for mastery of a highly melodramatic role. In 1971 Norman began working for her when she decided to return to acting after a few years' hiatus following the death of her second husband. "She had mellowed over the years," he told a writer about that time. "She was still very attractive, youthful-looking, and a pro. We didn't anticipate any problems getting her going again." And he was right. She still was a name to be reckoned with, and the years had apparently not dulled her abilities or her appeal. The press clippings from this period featured generally good reviews. Before too long, Susan's mounting health problems sadly began to undermine the comeback. But there was something just as damaging going on that wasn't in the newspapers.

A big part of Norman's job was to be the keeper of secrets. If he had ever lost his scruples and decided to do a tell-all, it would have made for seriously explosive reading. All his clients were human beings hardly immune from less than admirable attributes, some worse than others. All had skeletons in their closets, some closets more crowded than others. Generally, they were works in progress who had problems that could be solved as long they were willing to work on them. Others chose not to, and were holding a steady course on the road to self-destruction.

Susan Hayward, 1961, *Photofest*

Discretion and deference were given to a highly respected artist so as not to destroy her career in one fell swoop. The truth was that Susan was an alcoholic, and the situation had worsened dramatically, to the point where she was failing to show up for her commitments. She was heavily into Jack Daniels, according to her son Tim Barker.

At the same time, she was facing a more deadly threat—cancer, which was detected in her lungs and soon spread to her brain. (She was a two-pack-a-day smoker.) Additionally, there was much speculation that the filming of *The Conqueror* in St. George, Utah, in 1956 close to a nuclear bomb test site might have been the root cause. A disproportionately large number of the cast and crew of that film died prematurely of cancer, including John Wayne.

One of the first jobs Norman got for Susan's comeback was to star in *Auntie Mame*, a stage production at Caesar's Palace in Las Vegas. She was set to perform two shows a night, six days a week. Susan had never done live theater before but threw herself wholeheartedly into the project, working with a dance coach and a voice coach in New York. "Norman would go to Vegas and visit her and make sure she was doing okay," Tim recalled. "I think he probably knew my mother had a problem with alcohol. I don't remember the length of time that she worked on the production, perhaps around two months or so, when it started getting bad about her being present to do the show."

Norman and Susan's publicist, Jay Bernstein, called a press conference in Las Vegas to announce that Susan was leaving the show and Angela Lansbury would be replacing her. "Norman and Jay slid her out of it in a way that wouldn't have been embarrassing. They concocted this story that she had polyps on her throat. Had it become known that my mother had a problem with alcohol, it's very unlikely she would have ever worked again. Norman felt he had to protect her. If somebody had cancer or a drug or alcohol problem, the first move was always to keep it hidden because it would affect their livelihood. There was an impetus on the part of everybody to keep it quiet."

Norman set up Susan to do two television movies that were backdoor pilots, meaning that if they were well received, they could be developed into a weekly series. The first was *Heat of Anger* in 1972, a role originally cast for Barbara Stanwyck, but she got very sick and needed to be hospitalized. Norman flew to Mexico City to meet with Susan to delicately present the opportunity to her. To smooth over any hurt ego that she was not the first choice, Norman told her, "I'm sure that if Barbara had a choice of who she would want to replace her, it would be you." Tim told me that such sensitivity was hardly required. "One thing about my mother, she was realistic about where she was at that point."

Susan proved in her last forays that she could still deliver a stellar performance, but it is all tinged with sadness. Norman had seen it all—the extraordinary ascents and the horrible descents. He accepted it as an immutable part of the human condition. But it didn't make it any easier, especially when he had to confront his own deteriorating situation many years later.

Tim was very generous in sharing information about his mother that really brought home the complexities my father and all who work with great artists have to face. I felt that Tim was doing something Norman hated to do, sharing a secret. But it had a higher purpose, because it made me understand and feel enormous compassion for Susan Hayward and the illnesses and adversities she faced down. Tim left me with this story:

> "I was at Paramount with a client and my mother was working on a TV film on another set. I told my client that I was going to run over and see her. I walked into the soundstage and went up to my mother's trailer, which was parked inside it. She wasn't around. I asked some grip, 'Have you seen Ms. Hayward?' 'Yeah,' he said. 'I think she's down there behind those flats [large timber frames used for painted scenery].'
>
> "As I was walking, I heard someone sobbing. And on one of the backdrops, I saw only her hand. She was hidden behind it. 'What the hell is going on with you?' she goes. 'I can't do this. I can't do this. It's too fast. It's not like making a movie.' I called her doctor, and he came to the set."

Susan's doctor called Norman and shared with him in confidence that she was a dying woman. He was told not to accept any further offers for her.

CHAPTER 19

A Dog's Good Judgment

THE PHONE RANG AT THE SACRAMENTO RESIDENCE OF ARNOLD AND Leonore Spitz. Arnold picked up the phone and told Norman's assistant that his son was not at home at the time. Jumping on the line, Norman did his standard elevator speech about the Morris office and his background, going on to describe the magnitude of the moment and what he could potentially offer to expand it. The parents were suitably impressed.

Only a few days earlier, Arnold and Leonore's son Mark had captivated the American public unlike anyone since Neil Armstrong had walked on the Moon three years before. Mark Spitz had won seven straight gold medals at the Olympics, each in world-record time, over eight days ending on September 4, 1972. It was an unprecedented feat at the time, not to be duplicated until Michael Phelps thirty-two years later. There was little time for celebration, as the next day terrorists attacked the Israeli team, leaving seventeen people dead (including the five perpetrators). Since Mark was of known Jewish heritage, he was rushed home under tight security by the US State Department.

Those not yet born or too young to remember may draw a blank on his name, but most have seen the photo that would become one of the most iconic American sports images of all time. Hurriedly taken before changing planes in London, it showed the mustached Mark in his Speedo with the seven medals adorning his bare chest. During the session, an uncomfortably slippery layer of baby oil was applied to him for extra sheen, one he had no opportunity to shower off before the long plane ride home. He was paid $50,000 for the shoot by the German magazine *Stern*—a lot of money back then, which would help offset some of his upcoming college expenses at dental school. Sales of the poster of that famous image would earn him exponentially more. It was a portent of good things to come.

Like millions of others, Norman too was captivated by what he saw on television. Just as Mark's feat was unprecedented, equally so was that a top Hollywood agent would jump into the pool to represent an athlete. The fact that Mark was a swimmer made him seem all the less marketable. After all, aquatics were a low-profile sport, rarely seen outside of Olympic telecasts and ABC's *Wide World of Sports* series (known by its melodramatic catchphrase: "the thrill of victory and the agony of defeat.") Nor was watching people traverse a swimming pool a popular spectator attraction.

But Norman saw in Mark a transcendent figure beyond categorization, with all the makings of an iconic brand. It is baffling in retrospect that none of his peers had the same inspiration. In early twenty-first-century America, the boundaries between the business of sports and the performing arts have all but disappeared, with the affairs of superstar athletes commonly represented by the same mega agencies handling entertainment celebrities. The rare exceptions were sports figures who became actors, like *Tarzan*'s Johnny Weissmuller or ice-skating champion Sonja Henie decades before.

Norman was not the only interested party reaching out. Sports management pioneer Mark McCormack telegrammed Mark in Munich and later spoke with him on the phone when he had returned stateside. McCormack was an attorney, and lawyers handled most business affairs for athletes. In 1960 he started IMG, a mega sports management company that was ironically acquired by William Morris/Endeavor in 2013.

"He wanted me to drive to San Francisco to meet him," recalled Mark. He knew that McCormack was a giant in his field, representing all the big golf and tennis stars of that era. Mark explained that he didn't have a car and that he had to wait for his parents to get back to borrow theirs. Security was still a concern because of Munich, so much so that Governor Ronald Reagan was providing Mark with protection. Given all this, a trip to San Francisco would be complicated. Couldn't McCormack come to Sacramento since he was flying in from the East anyway, he suggested. "For some reason, he just couldn't find the time to do it," Mark explained. "And then I got a phone call from Norman."

The conversation after the one with his parents was not long-winded, which was not always the case with Norman, according to Mark. He told Mark how proud all Americans were of him and added the extra significance as one Jew to another. "Let me tell you a little bit about my agency if you don't already know," he said, condensing it to one easy serving. "You haven't signed with anyone yet?" he asked. "No, this is all happening so fast," Mark assured him.

The next day, Norman flew up and was sitting in the Spitz family living room in Sacramento. "We had this big Old English sheepdog, and Norman sat on the couch right where the dog normally sits," Mark laughed. "This big-ass dog like the shaggy dog in a Disney movie goes and sits in Norman's lap, you know, in all his dapper clothes. The dog didn't shed, but he really liked Norman." The dog's approval sealed the deal. "I'm going with Norman."

From the beginning, Norman provided a framework for success that was poetry in motion. Quickly, Mark was beginning to see far beyond earning a few dollars to offset his costs at dental school, which would soon fade as a career aspiration. "I never had any notion that there could be a possibility of marketing myself. And I didn't market myself. Norman did it. He had this understanding of how to keep the ball in the air. Part of it is illusionary. You throw stuff out there, and if it gets some momentum and traction, then there's a feeding frenzy. I call it persuasive blackmail. Norman was the expert at convincing the company that if they don't know quite what to do with Mark Spitz, then can they allow their competitor to figure that out?"

One of the first deals they inked was with Adidas, then only a shoe manufacturing company, to expand into swimwear. Mark and Norman put their heads together and decided as a general policy to not do endorsements as a hired pitchman. Licensing was the way to go they agreed, long before Michael Jordan and Nike appeared on the scene. It was a way to maintain an ownership of the product and forge more of a partnership.

Mark Spitz

"We're gonna get you $7 million," Norman predicted and promptly closed the deals—a lot of money back in 1973. Mark asked him to put him with the managers, accountants, and attorneys who handled William Morris's funds, which provided the foundation for his long-term financial well-being. "Norman was a one-stop shop," Mark explained. "It was epic in being able to look at him and trust him, and not to question whether he was full of shit. He brought a lot of credibility to me as a person, without me having to back it up. Every time he would bring me in to meet the people we were making a deal with, they were so excited about it that they couldn't actually sign it quick enough. There was obviously a lot of stuff behind the scenes to get to that point, but it was a reflection of Norman. I was the easy part to deliver. It was the credibility that he built, the trust that they would get the value for what it was."

The only part of the venture that did not come to fruition was ironically the entertainment piece, the most accessible resource in Norman's wheelhouse. Mark took acting lessons and was progressing well. One meeting at Universal epitomized the challenge he faced.

"In walked the nicest guy, Jewish-looking as all get-out. He was trying to get his movie off the ground. And my part was supposed to be in the water, the filmmaker explained. 'I don't have a problem with that,' I told him. He then said, 'Well, but in the movie, you're probably going to die.' I told him I didn't have a problem with that either." The filmmaker paused, suddenly realizing he had an unsolvable dilemma on his hands. He told Mark, "Yeah, but you're Mark Spitz. I can't kill you." The young filmmaker was Steven Spielberg; the film was *Jaws*.

"I was more famous than necessary. They could just never get past the fact that I was Mark Spitz." It meant that he was so identifiable, the audience would have a hard time accepting him playing someone else.

If a deal didn't go through, Norman was no different with Mark than with his other clients in always keeping a positive face. "He never said anything negative to me about why something didn't happen. It was always a positive spin and in the most delicately orchestrated way, in part to not have me think that he was failing or that I was failing, but it was the nature of the beast. I knew what he was talking about. As I told him on many occasions, 'You only saw me on eight days. You weren't part of my journey. I got a lot of friggin' medals that aren't gold and a lot of things that don't look like blue ribbons. That's who I am, and that's the character I have.' 'We'll come back and fight another day,' he would say.

And part of the reason I didn't get discouraged was that he made me a lot of money. I wasn't sitting there trying to find my next dollar."

Mark laughed about one opportunity Norman and he were examining right in the very beginning that they ended up passing on—an Anheuser-Busch beer distributorship. There was no use crying over spilt beer and the reality that someone like Frank Sinatra had made a ton of money from his distributorship, rivaling if not surpassing the wealth generated from his entertainment career. "Maybe had I been thirty years old at the time I would have done it, but I was only twenty-three. It wasn't the good-guy image I wanted to have. You know, it's okay to let some of those things get away. You don't catch the biggest fish every time you go fishing. But we were catching a lot of fish!

"Norman took me through the next twenty years of my life. In the beginning it was all exciting. There were two assistants in his office just handling [my] fan mail. But it made me understand that it was not going to last forever. And I was mature enough to understand that and appreciate what he brought to the table. He did it all in such a natural way that I don't think he consciously understood the impact that he had on us."

The Old English sheepdog had chosen well.

CHAPTER 20

The Agent They Let into the Oval Office

NORMAN WAS THE ULTIMATE MASTER AT "WORKING THE ROOM." THE singer Lou Rawls humorously described this activity as "spin and grin." Shyness was not one of Norman's shortcomings. If anyone within his radar range raised his curiosity, he would saunter over. The interaction was spontaneous and tailored to the moment, yet honed by decades of experience to create a powerful first impression.

The "room" could take many forms, including first-class airplane compartments, doctor's waiting rooms, and restaurants. At 21, New York's legendary watering hole, Norman had a special table reserved for him every time he was in the city. It was just to the right of the entrance to the main dining area. It was a smart strategy—anyone entering or leaving the place had to pass close by. To mark his spot, a replica of the William Morris logo hung from the ceiling right above his head, just one of a hundred other toys and trinkets dangling nearby—all of which probably had fun stories to tell.

Norman could even work a beach. A devout sun worshiper, he could multitask by tanning while schmoozing. For this purpose, Norman had a regular ritual of spending Sundays with colleagues and clients at Will Rogers State Beach in Santa Monica during a good portion of the 1950s and early 1960s. The Lastfogels sat in their beach chairs like the royalty they were. Sam Weisbord with his skinny legs power walked on the beach sipping carrot juice long before such practices were well known. Regrettably, I was often an involuntary participant, enduring the dual torture of boredom and a dreadful sunburn that resulted in a pervasive aversion to beachgoing. Getting skin cancer was not in his mind or anyone else's, as it was not part of the discussion back then. To the contrary, he always had a bronze tan on his face, helped along by a reflector—a folded piece of cardboard with silver foil covering one side to intensify the sun's rays. Zinc oxide ointment applied to his nose and lips and little white plastic eyecups were his only protection. Instead of sunscreen, he basted himself with a suntan lotion that smelled of coconut oil. Decades later, he had hell to pay at the dermatologist.

Santa Monica was replaced by the mid-1960s with regular trips to Acapulco, graduating in the early '70s to Hawai'i (always the Kahala Hilton, on the island of Oahu). The beach at the Kahala was a fantastic room to work. Famous companions on the beach included John Denver, Grace Kelly and Prince Rainier, and Happy and Nelson Rockefeller, among many others. There was also no shortage of industry friends and colleagues who also booked in at the same time, so Norman could have the best of both worlds—a wonderful change of pace geographically without any interruption of what he loved to do best: the high art of kibbitzing.

Unquestionably, one of the biggest payoffs of working thousands of rooms in his lifetime happened on the sands of the Kahala. On that day in the fall of 1976, Nelson Rockefeller and Norman lined their beach chairs together. The former governor of New York was at that moment the sitting vice president of the United States. They spoke at some length about President Gerald Ford. Although a lifelong Democrat, Norman expressed to Rockefeller his admiration for Ford, who was able to restore some sense of order and give the country a welcome respite from the turmoil of Nixon's Watergate scandal. Ford was up for reelection that November and faced an uphill battle.

Norman smelled an opportunity. Before they packed up for the day, Happy Rockefeller had given him First Lady Betty Ford's personal phone number. He had made up his mind to reach out when he was back at work at his office. But that call never happened.

That first day back, he opened the *Los Angeles Times* to see a story about President Ford and the preparation for an upcoming debate with Jimmy Carter. For all his down-to-earth demeanor, personal warmth, and obvious skills as a lawmaker, Ford was not known as Mr. Personality.

Working the beach with Prince Rainier of Monaco

Jokes abounded about his clumsiness, that he had played too many college football games without a helmet. The stakes were high for the debate, given the tightness of the race. It was still in the collective memory how John F. Kennedy had come off as attractive, articulate, and overwhelmingly charismatic in the televised debate in 1960 compared to Richard Nixon's sweaty lip beads, five-o'clock shadow, and ghoulish vibe. From that point forward, politicians did not want to repeat Nixon's mistake, even if it meant wearing makeup and getting serious media training from an acting coach—or, in Ford's case, one who also happened to be a comedy writer.

Norman peered at the photo accompanying the *Times* article and found his attention drawn to a person sitting across the conference table from the president. "I know that guy! That's Don Penny."

Kahala dinner with Happy and Nelson Rockefeller

There is an old show business adage once attributed to gangster actor George Raft: "The people you meet on the way up are the same ones you meet on the way down." It is just another form of "do unto others" or "mind your karma." If measured in units of karma, Norman had bank when it came to Don Penny.

Not everyone Norman handled was a household name, let alone a superstar. He recognized talent in his clients and did his utmost to market them. But sometimes, for factors not in his control, the product was wonderful but not everything turned to gold. And sometimes, as in this case, a "no" might lead to greater and very unexpected outcomes. In 1959 a young comedian and actor named Don Penny left New York to seek his fortune in Hollywood. He had an agent at the William Morris office in Manhattan who told him to call Norman upon arrival.

Don couldn't believe his luck. "Norman took me under his wing— and gave me not only the shirt off his back but several of his suits. I lengthened the pants a bit. At first everyone thought I was a William Morris agent." Norman even accompanied Don to many of his auditions, as if his very presence might improve the outcome. Don got some acting roles, including a regular gig in a short-lived 1965 TV comedy series called *The Wackiest Ship in the Army*, playing the ship's cook. Ultimately, Don ended up hanging his shingle elsewhere, applying his comedy-writing talents as an image consultant to help politicians and other public figures get their messages across with more humor. It had obviously worked, because Norman would soon be speaking with him—now the deputy director of communications for President Ford. Ford wouldn't be the last president Don knew. He did some writing for Ronald Reagan, including a notable joke about the assassination attempt—"Honey, I forgot to duck"—used at his Gridiron Dinner speech.

Memory decades later can be foggy, and it is unclear who called who first. But according to both, telepathy was in play. It appears that Don was already talking up Norman to President Ford around the same time as Norman was picking up the phone to call.

According to Don, Ford had confided in him about his worrying financial situation. "I don't have much money, and I wonder what I'll do if I'm not elected." Don replied, "I have someone I want you to meet. His name is Norman Brokaw." He explained to the president that Norman had access to corporations that paid big fees for speakers, among other avenues. The response was lukewarm at first, until Betty Ford chirped in and encouraged him. According to Don, she always had good common sense.

"Any relation to Tom?" "No, this Brokaw is the best agent in the business." "Shall I send him an airline ticket?" "Nope, I'm pretty sure Norman can find his way here if I call him."

The way Norman told it, he called Don and said, "I'd like to meet President Ford and talk to him." Don replied, "Norman, how is Thursday? President Ford has heard about you. He'd like to meet with you."

Forty-eight hours later, the door to the Oval Office opened and Norman and Don walked past Chief of Staff Dick Cheney. Ford was standing behind his desk and said, "Are you guys brothers?" "No, but I used to wear Norman's suits," Don replied. Norman was shown to a chair next to the president's desk.

"Lots of people come in here with problems," Ford told Norman. "It's nice to meet someone who may have solutions."

"I'm in the business of promoting people with talent."

"I'm not an actor. I can't sing or dance."

"Leave it to me."

According to an account of the meeting in the *Los Angeles Times*, Ford was quoted as finding Norman "very bright, very knowledgeable, and very aggressive." That same article had a humorous description of him: "Brokaw doesn't look the part of an agent. He's a short, carefully spoken, unflamboyant man who resembles a pharmacist more than he does a Hollywood operator." I wonder if they'd done the research and uncovered that his only other paid job in his lifetime was at a pharmacy in New York City as a young teenager. Very accurately, the writer also pointed out an obvious characteristic: "He seems fond of everyone he knows and fonder still of using superlatives to describe them."

A few weeks later, after the election was lost, they met again, this time at the Thunderbird Club in Rancho Mirage in the California

Norman working the Oval Office and pitching Gerald Ford

desert. Norman's pitch would provide the answer to the pressing question: "What do you do when you were the most powerful man in the world and now, suddenly, you are no longer?" They agreed that Norman would draft a comprehensive plan and that they would meet again in the White House in the waning days of the administration to take it to the next step.

It was of course not the first time Norman had ventured into unchartered territory outside of Hollywood. As mentioned earlier, he had signed Mark Spitz fresh after the swimmer had won seven gold medals at the 1972 Munich Olympics. The media landscape, although still quite analog in the 1970s, presented multiple avenues of opportunity, including books, endorsements, merchandising, speaking engagements, and network broadcasting, among others. The pioneering impact of a major Hollywood agency signing Mark Spitz broadened the field to include sports figures and other nonactor talent.

But representing a soon-to-be-former president of the United States was the top of the food chain. Up to that point, most former presidents more or less faded into the background as elder statesmen. Norman saw a parallel between Ford and Harry Truman, both soft-spoken, salt-of-the-earth Midwesterners who were vice presidents suddenly thrust into the highest office. Neither Truman nor any of his immediate successors had done much to add to their pension income beyond writing a memoir or taking a position in academia. Ford, however, did not want to just ride off into the sunset, nor could he afford to. Rather than taking a full-time position somewhere, he wanted to be involved only in a series of shorter term commitments he could pick and choose to his liking.

When he came to their final meeting at the White House, Norman was ready to present a plan he felt confident would preserve "the dignity and class of the presidency." According to Don, Norman told Ford, "Mr. President, I can't keep you in the White House, but once we carry out this plan, you can build a beautiful home wherever you want."

Ford liked what he heard: a book deal both for him and for Betty Ford, regular appearances on one of the television networks, and well-compensated speaking engagements—all designed to keep him fresh in the public eye and provide financial independence. Norman told

Ford that Betty's book would outsell his, and he was right—along with other revenue she would earn for public speaking and other appearances that helped build the Betty Ford Center. "Mrs. Ford joked that Norman got them a better deal than living at the While House," Don recalled.

As the meeting was concluding, Norman moved in for the close. "Mr. President, this is something I know I can do well. I'm going to New York from here. I'd love to be able to go in there and know that I am representing you."

Dean Birch, the attorney who was helping Ford during the transition, told him, "Mr. President, you're still in office. I don't think we should do it at this time."

"I want Norman Brokaw when he goes to New York tonight to know that he's representing the Ford family," Ford said firmly. "Send the communiqué authorizing it."

There was a telegram waiting for Norman at the front desk when he arrived at the Sherry Netherlands Hotel in Manhattan. The first deals started rolling in within seconds after Jimmy Carter took the oath of office. That day, Gerald Ford had a net worth of $300,000. A year later, that number was $12 million, all due to the deals Norman had generated. Norman told the Fords that the agency would represent them pro bono, but they insisted on paying the standard commission. They also offered to give Don a finder's fee, but he refused to take it.

Although literary agent Swifty Lazar had negotiated a book deal for Nixon around the same time, Norman's more comprehensive approach sent a powerful signal. It made everyone aware that people from the political world could be well represented by an agency across the board—not only in publishing but in other media as well. Before too long, other figures like Alexander Haig, Casper Weinberger, and C. Everett Koop signed with Norman—and even some nonpoliticians, like Armand Hammer.

One notable episode with Koop was one that Norman wished he could erase from memory. He had flown in with the former surgeon general to the headquarters of Procter & Gamble in Cincinnati to sign a contract. As Koop was about to sign, Norman noticed that the company had left off one of the zeroes at the end of the agreed dollar amount.

At that discovery, he immediately felt sick and soon doubled over in abdominal pain. The executives at P&G quickly brought in a bottle of Pepto-Bismol, one of their products, but it hardly did the trick. Soon after landing in Los Angeles, Norman checked in to Cedars-Sinai hospital with a nasty case of kidney stones.

With all that Norman accomplished in his career, there was nothing he was prouder about and had more fun doing than representing President Ford and his family. I always found it funny that among all the photos sitting in beautiful silver frames in his office were a few that were remembrances of things less than stellar. One that stands out above them all was a photo of him with Betty Ford walking in Red Square in Moscow, where he accompanied her on a promotional tour he had booked.

"It made me appreciate how well we had it in America," he told me. "The food was terrible, but the ice cream was great." True to his character was what he left out of the story, something he would never say in his lifetime that spoke in less than glowing terms about Betty or any of his clients. The food may have been terrible, but she clearly had enjoyed the Russian vodka, and lots of it. Soon after returning, the Ford family staged an intervention to deal with her addictions, one of the seminal events leading to her creation of the Betty Ford Center.

CHAPTER 21

The Prism

DONNA SUMMER CALLED NORMAN LATE ONE EVENING IN 1979. SHE was in New York, and with the time difference, he was still at his desk in Beverly Hills. She was crying hysterically. It wasn't a long conversation; Norman got the point. Before he hung up, he told her, "I'll be right there."

Donna was heartbroken. A promise had been broken on something very important to her, and it felt like a sacred trust had been violated. It came at a time of enormous popularity for her. She had just had two number ones on the Billboard Hot 100 ("Hot Stuff" and "Bad Girls") and soon would have one more with "No More Tears/Enough Is Enough"—a duet with Barbra Streisand. But before the last one was released, another single would come out that was of paramount importance to Donna both professionally and personally.

"Dim All the Lights" marked the first song that Donna wrote *alone*, both the lyrics and the music. "It was such a big deal for her," explained her manager and dear friend Susan Munao. "It was her moment to really establish herself, not just as a popular singer but as a singer-songwriter. It was a chance to go to a whole new level as an artist."

The single was released and was moving quickly up the charts. But despite his agreement with Donna, Neil Bogart, head of Casablanca Records, decided to release "No More Tears" a month earlier than he had promised. This move threatened to take the wind out of the sails of "Dim All the Lights," a tune that had every good chance to make it all the way to the top. It was a gut punch. It epitomized the kind of indignation that was galvanizing the nascent women's empowerment movement into a force for change.

Early that next morning, Norman knocked on the door of Donna's hotel room in New York City. He had taken the red-eye from LAX. He immediately handed her a small present he had brought with him on the plane. Inside the box was a prism-like piece of glass. It was a desk name plate engraved with the words "**DONNA SUMMER,** *CHAIRMAN OF THE BOARD.*"

The gift was not a rush job but premeditated, one he already had prepared in anticipation of this moment. Neither was it a novel idea that he had made up on the fly. The die had been cast a generation earlier when Loretta Young powerfully demonstrated to her young agent what could happen when women truly took control of their affairs and called the shots. If a client showed a similar inclination, Norman was only too eager to share the template.

Exhibit A on the wall of his office was a framed copy of an article in *Life Magazine* from the early 1960s featuring an impressive photo of Natalie Wood at the head of the conference table surrounded by men in suits, including Norman. The caption read, "Wood, a shrewd business-woman, enjoyed presiding over her high-powered cabinet."

From the way Donna described it, the desk plate with her name and new title engraved on it was a talisman. "When he came in and brought that prism, it was the beginning of my taking hold of my own life," Donna explained. "Had it not been for Norman telling me that I was allowed to take over my own life and that I was expected to take over my own life, I might still be running behind trying to catch up now. That was a pivotal point in my whole existence. That made me realize that not only did he believe in me, but that he expected me to believe in myself and to be an adult. I was not to be a child, not to allow people to walk all over me, and not to allow circumstances to invade me that I was not comfortable with."

What supercharged this moment was the fact that Norman had shown up in the flesh that morning, flying two thousand miles in the middle of the night for the sole purpose of delivering a small gift. In the grand scheme of things, it was a tiny investment of time and energy

Donna Summer

on his part. But it became a life-changing moment Donna would cherish for the rest of her days. It was not lip-service, some encouraging well-meaning sentiments said on a phone. Standing there in that hotel doorway, he told her more effectively than with words, "I believe in you. And I am here for you." And it wasn't because she was a great singer. It wasn't because she sold over one hundred million records. Those were just end products. Rather, it was all about her.

When I spoke with Susan to fill in some of the background about the episode with the prism almost forty-five years after, our voices began to crack with emotion as the conversation went on. I tried to put my finger on it, going first to all the sentimental places nostalgia can bring us. But I realized how unsatisfactory that line of thinking was. I was confident there was something far deeper to consider.

I wondered if moments such as this have been relegated to a quaint, bygone time, replaced by a new hyperrealism of a meaner era engulfed in fear, loathing, and greed. "They don't make them like him anymore," people are fond of saying about Norman, like they're talking about a species recently gone extinct. Small heroic acts of kindness still happen all the time, I assured myself. But do we all have within us what it takes to be as generous, unselfish, loving, caring, and ingenious as Norman had been that morning? "Just do the best you can," I heard Norman's wise voice coming in loud and clear.

It is also important to add what a remarkable example Donna set for us stemming from this moment. Gratitude is a spiritual practice all by itself. At a sold-out concert at the Hollywood Bowl many years later, Donna heartfully told the seventeen thousand people gathered there that there was a special person in her life in the audience and shared why. And later, at Norman's eightieth birthday celebration, she stood up and sang a tribute to him that no one who was there will ever forget: Gershwin's "Someone to Watch Over Me."

One postscript: Despite it all, "Dim All the Lights" made it to #2 on the Billboard Hot 100, with "No More Tears" at #1. Quality eventually and invariably always rises to the top. Donna was the first female artist to have two songs simultaneously charted in the top three, and this was the second time she had accomplished this feat.

CHAPTER 22

Speechless

As highly respected as he was, Norman could show signs of the mischievous schoolboy he once was. One afternoon he had a meeting at the Westwood home of a literary client, industrialist Armand Hammer. Norman had recently done a book deal for Hammer and was bringing over a stack of books as examples for him to review in preparation for writing his own work. Norman knew that he was scheduled on the heels of another meeting Hammer was having with Dr. Robert Gale. Gale was all over the news. The nuclear accident at Chernobyl had just happened, and Dr. Gale was the world's leading expert on medical response to such disasters. He had been summoned to the Soviet Union by Mikhail Gorbachev to lead the international team to help the victims.

Norman waited to walk up the path to Hammer's house to purposely cross paths with Gale. Just as they nodded hello to each other, Norman executed a perfect fumble and dropped the stack of books onto the brick walkway. Gale bent over to help him pick them up. Norman introduced himself and casually mentioned that these were all books his company had successfully negotiated. Mission accomplished. Several months later, Gale's book also would be added to that stack.

Norman was a firm believer in getting publishing deals for his clients. It wasn't about the money, although he always strove to negotiate the highest advance. It was really about the branding. The experience of holding a newly published, beautifully bound book written by one of his clients was a cultural event to celebrate. He knew that having the word "author" after their name brought prestige and credibility. If a celebrity name was big enough or the topic sufficiently newsworthy, it would generate a lot of buzz. Articles and reviews about the work would appear in the media, and authors could make the rounds of all the influential talk shows and do high-profile personal appearances and speaking engagements.

Norman's name was given to Nansci Neimann-Legette, a New York publisher, as someone who could help her company expand into celebrity books of substance. "'Make an appointment with Norman Brokaw, and if he'll see you, he'll give you a direction that you can follow,' I was advised," recalled Nansci. "We weren't the biggest publisher, but we happened to have a few successes."

Norman agreed to meet with her. He asked her what she was trying to accomplish. They had a nice chat brainstorming some ideas. A few days later, she received a note from him in the mail about how pleasant it was to meet her and hoping she would come back and visit with him the next time she was in California. Nansci wasn't sure if he was just being nice, since her impression at the time was that Hollywood really didn't care about New York publishing.

"He recognized that maybe there was an opportunity here, which triggered our friendship," Nansci explained. "I was very open to him suggesting ideas that were sometimes great, and sometimes they just didn't work for us. But the one thing I took away over the years was that he was always willing to have a conversation. Others will give you five minutes and go away. He never did that."

One such conversation was about the Betty Ford Clinic, which Norman had helped get started in the desert near Palm Springs. It had not been in operation for very long but was rapidly gaining acclaim. He wanted Nansci to come out and talk to them about doing a book.

"Well, okay, the next time I come out," Nansci began, only to be interrupted.

"No, you have to come out, and you have to come in and spend time at the clinic and see what they do," Norman replied.

Nansci ended up spending over a week observing the work at the clinic. Norman was right, and she went away convinced. They came back to meet with the director of the clinic and put forward an offer for the

Nansci Neimann-Legette

book. After all the effort and good faith expended, the director suddenly threw cold water on the deal. It wasn't about the money, he told them. Rather, it was about preserving what they felt was proprietary information. The clinic was still too new, and they needed to protect what they were doing.

"We both looked at each other. And I remember the look on his face. It was the only time I ever saw him speechless, without a suggestion of another way to go. Instead, his face said, 'I don't know how to get this done. I don't know where to go from here.'"

Nansci had one other surprise when she returned to New York. Seven days at Betty Ford? "Yeah, right, you were meeting them about a book? Nice try." The rumor mill had it that Nansci had gone to the clinic for personal rather than professional reasons.

One other book deal that didn't go through was that lovely bound book in Norman's office with the blank pages. *A Talent for People* was Nansci's brainchild.

CHAPTER 23

The High-Wire Act

PERHAPS ONE OF THE MORE FASCINATING THINGS ABOUT NORMAN HAD to do with his very unusual form of creativity. I think most of us limit the power of our imagination by not daring to let our minds venture too far beyond what feels familiar and safe to us. We think twice about sticking our necks out because we don't want to risk the shame of failure, looking stupid and being ridiculed in the process. Playing it too safe can dampen our creative intelligence. However, risks taken in an intelligent way, with lots of preparation, can manifest enormous rewards.

Norman did not have that inhibition. He was the kid who invented the fictious Jewish holiday to get off school. He was "signing dogs and cats" to jumpstart fictional television programming, and he acted on that off-beat hunch that created the prolific team of Sheldon Leonard and Danny Thomas. The list goes on. Norman believed in his abilities, and it gave him confidence and courage. Failures did not discourage him because they often led to better ideas, the rewards far outweighing the disappointments.

"Do you think you could walk a tightrope?" Norman asked Tony Orlando. He wasn't kidding. It wasn't a silly question but a real oppor-tunity Norman had in hand. And it turned out to be tailor-made for an artist who had achieved great success but had recently gone through traumatic (and very publicized) hard times.

Once a record company creative executive, Tony catapulted to fame as a singer with five number-one hits: "Tie a Yellow Ribbon 'Round the Ole Oak Tree," "Knock Three Times," "Candida," "My Sweet Gypsy Rose," and "He Don't Love You (Like I Love You)." "Tie a Yellow Ribbon" was the number-one Billboard song of 1973 and became Orlando's theme song. It grew into an American anthem of hope and homecoming, reunion, and renewal. His popular *Tony Orlando and Dawn* variety television show ran on CBS from 1973 to 1977.

Tony's downward spiral was triggered by grief in the wake of two deaths: his beloved sister Rhonda, who had cerebral palsy, and his best friend, comedian and actor Freddie Prinze, in late January of 1977. His depression, mixed with cocaine use over a nine-month period, resulted in a severe breakdown. He checked himself into what became a one-year stay in a mental hospital. After release, his agency at the time, ICM, put him on the road to perform under his own name without the two singers that had made up the group Dawn.

How Tony switched agencies and came to Norman and William Morris should be explained. Tony was close friends with the Ford family, specifically Betty and President Gerald Ford, before Norman met them. Tony had suggested that the president do a book and got his authorization to see if his agency would be interested in shepherding the deal. The response was ridicule and laughter. Cut to Norman, who asked to see Tony backstage at the Riviera Hotel.

"Tony, I understand you're friends with Betty Ford and Gerald Ford."

Tony nodded. "What are you doing with them?"

"Well, I've decided to do a book deal for the president. I really believe books from the greats of Washington is the future."

"Did he mention to you that I was going to take this to ICM?"

"He did. And I'm here to tell you, don't do it, because he's going to make the deal with me."

"Thank you for confirming that my instincts were right," Tony told him. From that moment, Tony decided to let ICM go and shortly announced that Norman was his new agent.

The offer Norman brought to Tony out of the gate was one of the strangest he had ever delivered to a client. "How would you like to audition for the lead role for *Barnum* on Broadway?" Norman explained that Jim Dale, the star of the show, was going on vacation, and they needed a replacement for two or three weeks in May 1981. No big-name actors would be willing to do it for such a short time, so there was an opportunity waiting.

The role would call for Tony to actually walk a tightrope. Norman's point was simple: "Tony, if you want to eliminate any speculation about being on drugs, how about if you could walk a tightrope?"

"I don't know."

"Well, if you can walk a tightrope, wouldn't you say that cleans up any suspicion about it? If you get the show, I'll be there in the wings with you on opening night."

Tony agreed and trained on the high wire at the Big Apple Circus. He then auditioned, got the part, and enthusiastically threw himself into preparing for the role. On opening night the music started for his entrance on stage, but there was no Norman. In the last second, Tony felt a little pat on his derriere. "Welcome to Broadway, young man," Norman said. "You're going to be a big star here."

Could Norman have known that this idea would be such a powerful catalyst to reshape Tony's life? Part of the ingenuity in this case was that it was delivered in an intriguing, bite-sized dose, something to which Tony was able to respond, "Yes, I can do that." He moved into action, a reset in taking back control of his life. And thankfully for Tony, the effect has endured.

Putting people into motion to help themselves successfully work through their difficulties is the mission of most social workers—and Norman perhaps could have had a successful career had he chosen that

Tony Orlando

field. Another classic story concerned a manager named Jeff Wald, who was married to Norman's client, singer Helen Reddy. Norman and Jeff had a highly successful collaboration, not only with Helen but with other shared clients as well. But Jeff had a massive cocaine problem. An overdose almost killed him.

"When an intervention was being done for me at Cedars-Sinai, and I virtually told the forty-odd people in my hospital room to fuck off, it was Norman who stayed behind," Jeff recalled. It was 1986, and Norman had Betty and Gerald Ford call Jeff to convince him to get treatment at Betty Ford. "I told Norman I didn't want to go 'because I couldn't use the phones.' Norman's pithy retort was 'There are no phones at Hillside Memorial' (the Jewish cemetery)." That sealed the deal. He went to the Betty Ford Center and ended up staying clean for the rest of his life, the next thirty-five years.

As Norman proved time and time again throughout his life, strong relationships are made from showing up and stepping up to help when the chips are truly down. It is easy to be a friend when the sky is blue and the sun is warm. If there was one life lesson to take away from these pages, it would be to appreciate how our smallest, seemingly unimportant actions of kindness and generosity given when others needed it most are more valuable than gold.

Dick Van Dyke perhaps put it best, speaking on a video tribute for Norman's eightieth birthday: "At William Morris, you were the most intelligent, the most fair-minded, the most honest. I and everybody trusted you a lot. And you did a lot of good for me too. But I think probably what I admire most in you is what you do outside the office, your humanitarian work. I don't know how many hundreds of people, including this one, who have come to you in time of need when there was serious illness in the family. And you were always right there, you get on the phone and leap into action the best doctors, the best facilities, the best treatment."

No drug could have made Norman feel higher than the satisfaction he got from helping others.

CHAPTER 24

"The Coach" Becomes "The Hornet"

OF ALL THE TWISTS AND TURNS IN A LIFE, THE MOST ABSURD ONE OF all concerned the greatest business success story of Norman's career that disintegrated in what can be described as a collapsing supernova (the explosive death of a massive star). If there is any poetic justice to be found, the gods saw fit that Norman never learned of the scope of the tragedy that befell his superstar client, who fell in popular opinion from America's favorite father to pariah.

Skeptical minds question how Norman could not have known. After all, his business relationship with Bill Cosby was very close and lasted more than fifty years, a virtually unheard-of longevity. Ask anyone in this orbit and they will affirm that Norman's cognitive health was so severely deteriorated by the time the rumors multiplied, he was spared learning of the magnitude of the accusations.

Over the entirety of his career, he hardly had his head in the sand when it came to clients behaving badly, human nature being what it is. He wasn't selling shoes but the talents of flesh-and-blood creatures who made stupid decisions just like everybody else. But add fame, wealth, power, glamour, and gossip to the mix, and it can quickly morph into a monster.

Most certainly, Norman was present as Bill Cosby's nearly squeaky-clean image took its first major hit in the aftermath of his son Ennis's death, when a young woman named Autumn Jackson claimed to be Cosby's illegitimate daughter. Norman had to deal with the fall-out as the pause button was hit on a good number of pending projects.

Damaging but not fatal, as such infidelity in Hollywood was hardly disqualifying or even eyebrow-raising, especially before the onset of the #MeToo era.

But the situation obviously did not stop there. Once comedian Hannibal Buress outed what had been a hushed whisper of severe sexual abuse allegations, there was nothing short of a pile-on effect. The magnitude was simply incomparable to anything Norman would have encountered over the breadth of his career. Had he been cognizant, he would have circled the wagons and gone into crisis management mode, at least in the beginning. But this was not the kind of thing he could have brushed away with his customary positive pep talk to clients that "everything happens for a reason" and "better things lay in store." He would have had no other choice than to make some resolute decisions and remain true to the ethics that had always been his North Star. But none of that came to pass. Dementia had already completed its work.

Despite deep friendships and genuine mutual admiration, Norman's relationship with his clients over the decades stayed within strict boundaries. If a client was going through some personal problem or health issue and sought Norman's advice and help, he gladly obliged. If that problem was adversely impacting the career, he might be more boldly proactive and put it on the table so the client would be fully aware of the potential consequences. But short of pleasantries about how the family was doing and what they might have done on their vacation, Norman did not stray unnecessarily into their personal affairs, especially when clients took extra measures to safeguard their privacy.

Most importantly, Bill went to great lengths to hermetically seal his personal life and protect his family from any violation of privacy. The realities of living with racism also dictated that the less people knew about his business and his holdings, the better off he would be. There were segments of society that took no delight in seeing an African American male become wealthy and powerful. His involvement in the civil rights movement and being singlehandedly responsible for the advancement of minorities in many fields of endeavor had taught him to take such preventative safeguards. The implications of being on Nixon's "Enemies List" alone could make any normal person paranoid, such as having the

Bill Cosby

IRS or the FBI sicced on him. Accordingly, in conversations both on the phone and in person, personal matters were not discussed unless Bill or Camille brought up the subject themselves.

Unlike many of his contemporaries, Bill eschewed having an entourage. On the road, he was quick to excuse himself to go to his hotel room after a performance. And often, thanks to his private jet, he would beat a path to the airport. Early on, the family moved to rural western Massachusetts to raise their five children in a protected bubble far from the media glare.

These boundaries were all well-defined and respected. The agency and all its related service entities, including production staff, attorneys, accountants, insurance agencies, and the like, were focused on keeping their star client happy. The attention and loyalty were reciprocated in the form of gifts—fun and spontaneous small gestures and perks that demonstrated Bill and Camille's respect, appreciation, and gratitude for those at the higher echelons. Great agents were hard to find; integrity and trust were even rarer. Norman always described the Cosbys as being the epitome of class (especially when speaking about Camille), and neither party ever let down their guard to cause any fissures in that facade—at least while Norman was still healthy and actively on the case.

The Cosby-Brokaw partnership got off to a roaring start in 1964 thanks to Sheldon Leonard, all traced back to that notorious chimp that climbed up the lamppost on Canon Drive a decade earlier. The situation was not so transactionally crass that Norman had "to call in a favor" with Sheldon. But it was a credit to the strong relationship they had forged, in which reciprocity was respected and never abused.

Marty Litke, an agent in the New York office, was raving about a young comedian who was playing at the hungry i, a nightclub in San Francisco. Enrico Banducci's historic North Beach venue helped launch the careers of Lenny Bruce, Barbra Streisand, Jonathan Winters, Joan Rivers, the Smothers Brothers, and Woody Allen during its heyday in the 1950s and 1960s. Popular African American comedian Dick Gregory had been playing there but wanted to take some time off. He was getting more and more active in the civil rights marches in the South, so he suggested that a young comedian from Philadelphia could fill in for him. It was the first time Norman heard about Bill Cosby.

"From the moment I met Bill Cosby, I noticed a lot more than the obvious fact that he was as funny as a human being could possibly be," Norman explained. "What I also felt from that first impression was a genius and a talent that I knew could forge an outstanding career in this business. I was right. And it happened very quickly."

At this same time, Norman got wind of a new show that NBC had just bought called *I Spy*. It was to star Robert Culp and an African American actor as a couple of American Defense Department agents masquerading as "tennis bums" who traveled the world on adventures to chase villains, spies, and women. Culp's partner was slated to be a well-known African American actor who would function as an older mentor. Most importantly, it would be a historic first: An African American would have an equal co-starring role with a White actor on network television.

The show's executive producer happened to be Sheldon Leonard. He informed Norman that the casting of Culp's co-star was close to being finalized but not yet sealed.

"From everything I've heard, you really have to meet Bill Cosby," he told Sheldon. He agreed, so Norman arranged for Bill to showcase his act at a club on the Sunset Strip called The Crescendo. Sheldon liked what he saw and called Norman the next day. "What do you want me to do," he asked.

"Sheldon, it's very important if we can get the role for Bill Cosby," Norman said. "It would be great if you could give him the opportunity."

"You got it."

But it wasn't as easy as that. There was another major hurdle to overcome. NBC said their Southern affiliate broadcasters were balking at the progressive racial statement the show was going to project. For the first time on American television, race—literally and figuratively—was not going to matter. Bill Cosby as "Scotty" and Robert Culp as "Kelly" would be equals and would treat each other accordingly. It was to be as momentous for television as it was for Major League Baseball when Jackie Robinson integrated the sport.

NBC was worried that the show would not be well received in the South. Their top executives at the time, Herb Schlosser and Mort Werner, flew out from New York to meet Bill Cosby in Norman's office. Sheldon and Norman held their ground. If they wanted the show, it had to be with Bill Cosby. Fortunately, the execs agreed and were promptly rewarded. *I Spy* was an immediate sensation. Audiences responded to the special chemistry between Culp and Cosby. Given the societal turmoil in the wake of the civil rights movement of the 1960s, it was the right show for the right time. And Bill Cosby was the right person for that time.

With the exposure from the hit television show, Bill Cosby quickly became a huge star, a force in the business, as Norman had predicted from the beginning. Not everything Bill touched had the same fairy dust that made *I Spy* a breakout success. But hits and duds aside, Bill had built the kind of multimedia platform few of his peers had enjoyed. It seemed that no matter what he did from that point on—from live performances to comedy recordings, films to other television series, legendary comedy albums to record-shattering best-selling books, and, last but not least, commercial endorsements like Jell-O and Coca-Cola—Bill Cosby quickly became the force in the business that Norman had envisioned from the beginning.

But absolutely nothing could match the impact of *The Cosby Show*, which ran on NBC from 1984 to 1992. In the decade prior, he had taken a break from doing a television series since none of the attempts since *I Spy* had had much traction. The box office from a string of motion pictures was mostly decent, but it didn't propel that facet of his career into overdrive.

Eventually the discussions of going back to television heated up. The idea had been broached a few times but had fallen on reluctant ears, dismissed as "not being the right time." That all changed. Bill wanted to ease up on his live concert work and be closer to his family. He also saw a lane open to do something more meaningful on television than the program offerings of the time. Parenthood had been a rich well of material for his comedy routines and could do likewise for a situation comedy series.

So Norman went to work, introducing Bill to producers Marcy Carsey and Tom Werner, who had established themselves as hitmakers at ABC Television and had recently struck out on their own. Bill had decided that the show would be set in a working-class environment. But instead of portraying a chauffeur, Tom and Marcy convinced him to make his character an obstetrician and his wife a successful lawyer. It would become the first American television show to feature a prosperous upper middle-class African American family with a two-parent household. Many celebrated this factor for breaking racial stereotypes and changing social attitudes that had previously limited images of upward mobility.

Bill was very fond of bestowing nicknames on some of his close associates. Norman had originally been called "Coach," harkening back to Bill's days on the track team in school. As they left the big meeting with NBC to finalize the deal for *The Cosby Show*, Norman walked out with a new name. Religiously punctual, Norman had been uncharacteristically a few minutes late. As the participants waited for him, they were all smiles and laughs, chatting amicably among themselves. But when Norman entered the room, the lighthearted mood changed abruptly. His arrival meant it was time to get down to business. "It was as if a hornet had entered the room," Bill explained. From then on, Norman was known as "The Hornet."

In the early years of *The Cosby Show*, it was estimated that sixty-two million viewers tuned into the program every Thursday night. Police departments commented on how quiet their 911 phone lines were and how crime rates went down when the show was on. It was also an enormous business success, the first property to ever generate $1 billion in syndication sales. Carsey-Werner soon had the top-three television shows in the country with *The Cosby Show*, its spinoff *A Different World*, and *Roseanne*. And so enormous was his popularity, it seemed that everything Bill Cosby touched turned into gold.

The revenues Norman generated for William Morris during the 1980s and 1990s (thanks in great measure to his work for Bill Cosby) were credited by many for singlehandedly keeping the business in good health at a time of downturn. Moreover, a generous portion of the wealth was invested philanthropically by Bill and Camille, especially in education, civil rights, the arts, and social justice. Most notably, hundreds of young African Americans received full college scholarships. For many who were involved in these charitable causes, myself included, the downfall of Bill Cosby is extra tragic, since so much force for good was obliterated in its wake.

Anybody with a well-rounded education can find any number of analogies to describe what transpired. Those versed in the classics might talk of the fatal flaw at the core of Greek tragedies—"hubris," the pride that blinds. Historians can point to the impermanence of dynasties and the rise and fall of empires. Social scientists might launch into a discourse on the illusion of fame and how the masses delight in schadenfreude, proving spitefully that celebrities are no better than we. Physicists might speak of how gravity and the elements of nature inevitably reduce the edifices of humankind into rubble and dust over time. Time has not healed all wounds. There has been no second act.

CHAPTER 25

Don't Touch the Hair

"THE LAST THING WE NEED IS ANOTHER VIP COMING IN HERE." MAR-guerite Longley was the head nurse of the eighth-floor section of Cedars-Sinai hospital. There had been a lot of difficult patients and cases, and all the nurses were exhausted. "He's a very nice man," the head of Patient Relations implored, explaining that the newcomer was having cataract surgery the following Tuesday. Marguerite promptly forgot all about it.

"On no, she did it anyway," Marguerite muttered to herself, seeing Norman walking down the hall and into his room, escorted by Barbara and Jules. The gurney was outside the room, waiting to take him to the operating room, the anesthesiologist was ready to sedate him, Norman was on his cell phone in some negotiation—all while he still hadn't completed the admission process. Donning her authoritarian hat, she told him, "Mr. Brokaw, you can't do that. Give me the phone."

While Norman recovered from the surgery, Barbara got to know everybody on the floor, including Marguerite. Barbara told her father the next day that the head nurse was "single and decent," a tag that teasingly stuck to her for a while among her colleagues. Later that same day, he needed to go to the treatment room to get his eyepatch bandage changed, but there wasn't any spare staff available. So Marguerite pushed him in the wheelchair, waited for him patiently, and then wheeled him back to the room. To thank her, Norman took some Donna Summer recordings from his leather bag and gave her a couple as a gift—and then he asked for her phone number. She hesitated. She had never gone out with a patient before, plus the age difference would give anyone pause. So he gave her his phone number instead. Not short on confidence, he told her, "If you can't reach me at this number, call me at that one."

"So I went out with him. We went to Chasen's and sat at his special table; he showed me his house up the hill from there in Trousdale and then drove me home to Santa Monica. He talked and talked and talked, and I don't think I said three words—just kidding. And then he kept calling me and calling me." The courtship moved into high gear with the same care and fastidiousness of Norman the deal closer. One early highlight was a trip to Rancho Mirage to hang out with Gerald and Betty Ford.

Cut to a few months later. Norman called her at work: "Meet me at the Beverly Hills Hotel at three." He had champagne waiting, and two diamond engagement rings for her to choose from. She was in a state of shock. Neither of the lavish rings he had picked out were to her taste, so she selected the one she disliked the least.

The engagement lasted a total of nine days. Norman knew what he wanted, and he always moved quickly once he made up his mind. There was no time to lose, and no time like the present. They were married at the high-rise condominium off the Sunset Strip belonging to Sam Weisbord. Los Angeles County Superior Court Judge Laurence Rittenband, Norman's friend, officiated. Rittenband was also known as the Polanski judge, since he presided over the controversial child molestation case that led to the film director's flight into exile.

According to the adage, "The third time is the charm," and in this case, marriage number three proved happily to be the case for Norman. Or, as Marguerite put it, "I would say to him, 'I may be your third wife, but I'm your last, and don't take that as a threat.'" Fundamentally, what set this relationship up for success was the level playing field in their power dynamics. As accomplished as Norman was in his field, so was Marguerite in her work. She had one of the most coveted jobs at Cedars-Sinai, and it was no fluke that she had risen to that position. She was the whole package—a compassionate and caring person (true to the nature of her profession) and a consummate patient advocate, while also having the ability to stand her ground when dealing with complex personalities.

Those qualities would be put to great use in the marriage as the years rolled by.

"The thing that worked about the marriage was that he had his life, and I had my life," Marguerite explained. "If I wanted to go somewhere on my own, from going by myself to the movies or on a trip with my family without him, I could go. And if he wanted to go to New York, he could. We weren't clingy with each other."

Marriage with Marguerite in 1983 coincided with a wave of good fortune. Norman's career achievement was at its peak. *The Cosby Show* debuted on the airwaves and set off a domino effect of prosperity. Norman's age had started to mellow him in his midfifties. He still had the energy and drive to excel that he displayed his first day in the mailroom, but with less urgency. He still looked forward to coming into his office every morning. But he could take his foot off the accelerator to relax a little more and better enjoy the ride. Much of what he had set out to do

Norman and Marguerite

had been accomplished. The prophecy uttered to his young date some forty years earlier of someday running the place was well on its way to coming true. He would be named president and chief executive officer of William Morris in February of 1989. Exactly two years later, he assumed the title of chairman and CEO.

When their daughter, Lauren, was born in 1985, Norman enjoyed family life more than ever before. The joke was that Lauren had a father and a grandfather all in one with him. He was as equally hands-off with the nitty-gritty of early childhood parenting as he had been with his previous five children, never once changing a diaper. Given the easygoing independent spirit of their relationship, this was never a source of marital discord. In fact, the only conflict they had was when Marguerite felt that Norman's protective support of Barbara was enabling some of her destructive behaviors. Norman felt so badly for Barbara that he rarely raised his voice toward her. One notable exception was when she threw her dirty underwear over the fence into Senator Kuchel's yard. Kuchel's German shepherd dog had a menacing presence as Barbara went over to collect it. Marguerite said she had never heard such outrage and profanity from Norman's mouth.

Thanks to their healthy relationship and the sound boundaries they established, Marguerite was able to make her views clear and resolve most issues before they became flashpoints. "I tried to intervene a lot with Barbara to get him to put some kind of discipline in her life. She needed discipline, because he more or less let her do whatever she wanted. I also tried to help him with Wendy because he had a kind of a bad relationship with her at times—caught in the crossfire of the divorce. I tried to get him to understand her point of view. Sometimes he also thought I could be too strict with Lauren."

Norman listened when Marguerite put her foot down regarding a second home they had purchased in Palm Desert. The charm of that lifestyle quickly wore thin with torturous, traffic-clogged weekend commutes and other downsides that made it stressful and hardly worth the trouble. He also wanted to go there in August, when it was 116 degrees in the shade. The house was promptly sold.

Jules was also exiled as the gopher-in-chief when Marguerite grew fed up with the growing list of dysfunctional incidents instigated by Barbara, with Jules as the terrorized target. The worst was when she stole his false teeth and threw them to the bottom of the swimming pool. On family trips, Barbara would frequently burst into his room in the middle of the night to scare him. Enough was enough.

Lauren never saw the harsher, controlling, fear-inducing side of Norman that her older half-siblings had. As she grew older, they became partners in crime, and she would be his frequent companion at industry events, which held waning interest for Marguerite. "Before he came down for breakfast, he would take out a shirt and try several ties, placing them around the collar to see which one looked best," Marguerite recalled. "I was never consulted, because I didn't have any style. He would always call Lauren, and they would discuss the topic at length and decide which one looked the most perfect.

"We got along really well," Marguerite explained. And in the few instances they didn't, she had a great method to resolve it. "If he was upset about something, he would sulk. He wouldn't talk. So then I would say, 'Okay, you're not talking. Can you give me an approximate time and date when you're going to start talking?'" Norman had met his match.

From my distant observation post, Norman was far more relaxed and accessible with Marguerite in his world than I had ever experienced him. Get-togethers at Thanksgiving or for Father's Day were suddenly something to truly look forward to rather than an obligation. The inclusion of Marguerite's side of the family at these occasions added to the enjoyment.

His life at the office also settled into a type of parallel domestic bliss, and a major reason was having Mary Feinberg as his trusted assistant. From their first interactions, there was something in her that triggered his talent sensor. She was an assistant to Sam Weisbord the last nine months of his life, placed in that role for good reason. Sexual harassment in the workplace had become a major liability but not yet ripened to a level of zero tolerance, and Sam's aggressive manner with women and resulting accusations had become a flashpoint. Lawsuits from two former assistants were still pending at the time of his death several years later.

Mary was deemed a safe choice for that role, given that Sam refused to have a male secretary. She was happily married but also rock solid in her personality. Norman told her that one day she would work for him, and he made good on that promise once Mary was available. The first day, he told her that she worked *with* him, not *for* him, and that was the spirit of their relationship for the next twenty-five years.

"It was a funny thing about Norman that whenever we went out for lunch or dinner, he would never order dessert," Mary recalled. "'I don't have dessert,' he would always tell the waiter. But he would want you to order dessert so he could have a piece of it."

What remained a constant was the all-encompassing passion he had for life as expressed through his work, and it spilled over to dominate his social life. Fortunately, this was also something Marguerite accepted with no reservation. Anytime they went out, it was always related to business, his clients, and his company. She never demanded reciprocity, for the two of them to go out with some of her friends or colleagues.

What were these meals like? Sue Cameron, Kim Novak's manager, who would frequently have lunch with him at Spago or Hillcrest Country Club, put it succinctly: "He was like a little boy with a train set. His eyes always sparkled with the enthusiasm of a six-year-old with every new client and project. Even as he grew weaker, he was always ready to relive and talk about his wonderful life. I thought of Norman as my uncle. What I remember the most was his true love of the business."

Marilyn McCoo and Billy Davis Jr., who Norman helped chart their solo careers after their years with the highly popular singing group The Fifth Dimension, cherished breaking bread with Norman and Marguerite. "He'd call us and say, 'Hey, I'm going to go to the club; let's meet for dinner, I'll see you over there,'" Marilyn recalled. Billy added, "It wasn't a show business experience. It was more like friends getting together, hanging out, talking about our lives. We wouldn't even bring up anything that was happening in the business unless it was something really important."

"He was fun; he had lots of energy," Marguerite said. "He had more energy than I had. He had this thing about anyone touching his hair. So, just to tease him, I'd reach over in the car and put my hand on his hair on purpose. I couldn't help it. And he'd always go, 'Don't touch the hair!' I guess I wanted to irritate him.

"As time went on, he and I started to say no to going out. We just wanted to stay home. If we had an invitation to some event, we'd say, 'Do we really want to go?' And then we'd wait around for a couple of hours before we'd both say, 'No, let's not go.'"

Perhaps the highest compliment Marguerite could give Norman was after his passing. "My friends have said to me in recent years, 'Don't you want a boyfriend? Don't you want to get remarried?' And I say, 'No, I don't want a boyfriend or a husband. Why would I? How could I ever duplicate this? I had the best, so I'm not looking.'"

CHAPTER 26

Genius Loves Company

"HOW DID IT COME ABOUT THAT YOU AND I ARE SUCH GREAT FRIENDS," an elderly Norman asked Berry Gordy, the man who brought the magic of Motown to the world. They had been working together for almost five decades at the time.

"Because everyone else is dead," Berry replied. Berry was only two years younger than Norman, but their laughter was evidence of the good fun they had together, especially as they had gotten older.

The fact that they were great friends is not as unlikely as it might seem. Both possessed the extraordinary gift of recognizing talent and, most importantly, knowing what to do with it. Despite their different backgrounds, they both spoke the same language and shared much in common.

In Norman's case, it is hard to imagine what American culture would look like without Marilyn, Elvis, and that novelty called TV, which grew into the most power medium thanks in no small measure to Norman's behind-the-scenes contributions. And what Berry Gordy accomplished with Motown is unquestionably one of the most revolutionary impacts of the popular arts on American society in the twentieth century.

We baby boomers who were alive and halfway socially aware in the volatile 1960s could turn on the evening news to see the civil rights movement in action: Martin Luther King Jr., the speeches, marches, strikes, riots, firehoses, and billy clubs. Turning the channel, we might find a different face of the movement—softer and more subtle, infectious, and irresistible, but a very powerful statement all the same. Music did the talking and the persuading. Diana Ross and the Supremes, the Temptations, Marvin Gaye, Martha and the Vandellas, Gladys Knight and the Pips, the Jackson Five, Stevie Wonder, the Four Tops, Smokey Robinson and the Miracles, and many other Motown artists appeared frequently on the popular Ed Sullivan show and other top rated television network programs.

Berry Gordy brought a powerful transformational message of what might happen if America's diversity could be truly embraced instead of feared and reviled. He saw Motown much like the world Dr. King was fighting for: people of all races and religions, working together harmoniously for a common goal. In fact, Berry talked about how Dr. King said the two of them were on the same path: While Dr. King was trying to bring about political and intellectual integration, Motown music was already bringing about emotional and social integration.

Little time had passed since American pop music had been segregated just like housing, schools, hotels, and shops. With rare exceptions, African American recordings were mostly played on "Negro" stations and referred to as "race music." Artists like Nat King Cole, Louis Armstrong, and Sammy Davis Jr. had broken barriers, but Motown truly opened the floodgates to the mainstream. The excitement of White audiences for this product brought unexpected benefits. There was not today's plethora of pop music genres or so many media outlets or technologies where the music could be heard. So the broad acceptance of Motown translated into sizable exposure on mainstream radio and television programming—and its music found an eager audience, especially among younger non-Blacks who wanted a new beginning and a departure from previous generations' legacy of racism. I was one of them, taking the bus to UCLA at age fourteen to see the Supremes live in concert in 1967 in their flowing chiffon dresses. It was the right music for the right time.

When Berry moved from Detroit to Los Angeles in 1972, Norman was there as his trail guide to help expand Motown's platform to film and television. "Norman was a first timer," explained Berry. "There was never a strike one or a strike two. The first people he introduced me to always turned out to be magical. I will always be grateful to Norman for his great insight. Whenever I'm praised or get compliments, I always think about where it started and who helped me when I needed it the most. And Norman's name always comes up. For almost fifty years, I witnessed his kindness, loyalty, passion, dedication, humanitarianism, and deep love for his fellow man. He was the secret driving force behind the many of us fortunate enough to have him in our lives."

When he set out to make *Lady Sings the Blues*, the motion picture on the life of Billie Holiday starring Diana Ross, Berry told him with trepidation that he had never done a film before. "Don't worry, I've got connections," Norman replied and immediately put him together with director Sidney Furie and producer Jay Weston. The film went on to receive five Oscar nominations, including best actress and original screenplay.

Berry recalled, "He told me about Hollywood, how it was then and how it is now. It was fascinating to hear all about Marilyn Monroe and Kim Novak and the rest of his roster, all these beautiful women I had a crush on. That's why I never grew tired of listening to his stories, no matter how many times I heard them."

Above all, Berry credits Norman for an otherworldly ability—call it gut or intuition or a knack of instinctively knowing people—to know what they could do and with whom they could best collaborate. "He even told me he knew what his clients wanted before they did." Berry was skeptical hearing that until Norman started doing the very same for him. "I was just so amazed."

The story of this enduring friendship is in many ways perhaps the most inspiring of all of Norman's accomplishments in my mind. It is the relationship I knew the least about, since Norman shared few if any details about his work life with me unless he had good reason. I can't say that I even knew that Berry Gordy was his client until well into Norman's final years. Once my brothers and I started working in the industry, we found opportunities to collaborate with Norman, and the information flowed a little more freely. My brother David once humorously remarked, "Our father is our client."

Berry Gordy is hands down an extraordinary genius. And it spoke volumes that he chose Norman as his trusted advisor over the decades. Norman was fond of saying that the main attribute of genius is simplicity.

Berry Gordy

We may misguidedly think that simplicity sounds like "simple" and, therefore, easy. But it is anything but. Our minds are so incredibly cluttered and distracted that we often fail to see the simplicity when it stares us in the face. Where Berry saw in Norman a power of premonition, it could also be considered an exercise in simplicity—cutting through the clutter, going straight to the core, and recognizing the truth. It is a form of genius that can easily go unrecognized.

CHAPTER 27

The Changing of the Guard

WITH THE BEGINNING OF THE NEW MILLENNIUM, IT WAS CLEAR THAT more had changed than the clocks and calendar. It felt like the time had also expired on the kinder, more polite world with all its niceties, be they superficial or sincere. One could not ask for a more fitting symbol for the pivot to a more mean-spirited and crueler mentality than the debut of reality television in 2000 and *Survivor*. In contrast to people working together for the common good, it was all about using one's creativity and cunning to vanquish others. Nice guys tended to finish last. "What's in it for me" became the mantra for the new era.

Unceremoniously, the portraits of founder William Morris and Abe Lastfogel were removed from the walls of the spacious lobby—a newer generation of leadership felt the organization needed a major facelift. Telling the glorious history of Hollywood and all the old stars that younger people hardly knew felt out of touch. That along with some other softer aspects of Norman's persona were suddenly judged anachronistic. Ironically, the decision-maker who removed the portraits did not last long in the position—divine retribution perhaps?

The pace of life had sped up dramatically, fueled in large measure by the growth of the emerging internet, social media, and other new information and communications technologies. Going the way of the dinosaurs were the old office machines—the typewriters, Dictaphones, stenographer pads, telex machines, overnight mail pouches, metal filing cabinets, Rolodexes, stereo hi-fis, and tape players. Even the fax machine, once heralded as a modern marvel, came and went in a flash. This

The portraits of William Morris and Abe Lastfogel with the old logo, just before their removal from the lobby

machinery made the office run over the many decades Norman worked at the agency. And now it was all being thrown away. The same could soon be said of Norman himself.

By the stroke of midnight starting the new millennium, the generational shift had already been underway for some time. A lot of it was entirely appropriate and encouraged. Every great organization needs to regularly reinvent itself, to adjust and keep up with the changing times. Mergers and acquisitions were a welcomed infusion to revitalize tired blood. You had to keep your feet moving or risk being overrun by the competition closing the gap. Each time such a big move was considered, Norman gave a full-throated endorsement.

The final merger during his time was more dramatic; the venerable old name of the company, in use for well over a century, was being altered as a result. The distinctive superimposed "W" and "M" that made up the logo was being dumped as well. It felt akin to suddenly discarding the American flag for a new one. When I asked Norman what he thought about it, his response was not what I expected. He was totally down with it, a small sacrifice in his mind to the potential upside. He knew very well that this was not a business to rest on one's laurels, including the reputation of the old name and venerable logo. It was totally a "what have you done for me lately" kind of business.

Truth be told, there had been a vacuum at the top for quite some time. Norman had done an outstanding job as CEO and later chairman, keeping the ship afloat with all the revenues from Bill Cosby–related enterprises in the 1980s and early 1990s. But a good portion of the old politburo had already gone to their final resting places at Hillside Memorial Park in Culver City, including Mr. Lastfogel, Sam Weisbord, and Morris Stoller, who all died within a three-year period in the mid-1980s. Others in the previous leadership had seen the handwriting on the wall and had exited; some joined other agencies, started their own enterprises in management and production, or simply retired. Norman and a few others stayed. "Retirement is not a word in my vocabulary," he was fond of saying.

Much to his detriment, Norman did not have a Plan B when it came to a life outside of William Morris. It is a fair assumption that he did not

The old guard: Abe Lastfogel with Sam Weisbord, Morris Stoller, Norman, and Joe Schoenfeld

have the fire in his belly to reinvent himself in his golden years. By 2000, he had been at the same company for fifty-seven years. If he had been an agent giving career advice to Norman the client, he would have told him that it was high time to move on and move forward. But he would have been speaking to the wall. No man loved his job more than Norman. It continued to be all-enveloping, and there were still enough trappings of his personal power intact, at least for the time being.

It is also important to note that Norman did not have any hobbies or extracurricular activities that he was passionate about and could have filled the void. He neither gardened, collected art (to any serious degree), delighted in wine or other culinary arts, or traveled to new or exotic locations. And remember his brief foray into trout fishing in the 1950s? He did play tennis at the country club for exercise and some socializing. He also loved following the Dodgers baseball games on television but had stopped going to sporting events in person decades before. At most, he loved being at home with his family and dogs and going to nearby restaurants and occasional entertainment industry events.

As underscored before, there were any number of other career opportunities he could have explored but chose not to consider. In a heartbeat he could have exited the company and opened his own personal management firm. Every one of his top clients, without exception, would have followed him, their loyalty far greater to Norman than to William Morris. And there is no question that it would have been a highly lucrative move, pocketing the 10 percent or possibly higher for himself instead of taking a smaller share after depositing it into the company coffers. He had the name and reputation to pull it off. Anyone of note was always quick to return his phone calls.

So many owed him a debt of gratitude for myriad reasons, for small kindnesses never forgotten to major life-changing and sometimes life-saving favors. His generosity was heartfelt and earnest, even though it frequently translated into stronger relationships that impacted the bottom line. As previously mentioned, an area in which he took special delight was helping people facing health crises get the best care available through his carefully curated network of top medical specialists. Being on the board of Cedars-Sinai Medical Center was one of his gateways to this expertise.

"Are you related to Norman," I have been asked hundreds of times. Those asking would almost always share stories of the extraordinary goodwill he had generated, especially in the health arena. Of all those times, the one I will never forget happened when I had to travel from Los

Angeles via London and on to the Cannes Film Festival in the south of France in the late 1990s. A person had died on the plane before the flight departed, which understandably caused a big delay. A few others on the flight had the same itinerary and would also miss the only connecting flight from London to Nice. One of my fellow passengers was Jeff Berg, head of ICM, an intense rival of the Morris office. When he saw I was similarly impacted, he told me, "We're chartering a private plane. You're coming with us." He explained that some time ago, Norman had heard about his mother's illness and got her the help she needed. Karmic debt repaid, so to speak.

Just as the book with the blank pages was not destined to be written by him, Norman never gave serious consideration to leaving the company. He might have fantasized about it on a particularly frustrating day, but never would it evolve any further. The loyalty and longevity of his relationships with his clients was no different from how he felt about the firm.

It was perhaps also a quixotic attachment to the good old days. That gentler, kinder, slower paced world of Norman's generation in the twentieth century was the beneficiary of a roll-up-the-sleeves, optimistic grit had helped America overcome the Great Depression, defeat fascism, build the interstate highways, and put a man on the Moon. There was a sense that they were building a better world, and the sky was the limit. Just as people teamed up to accomplish those impressive feats, the employees of the Morris office were rewarded handsomely if they bought into the system and invested their time and creative energy. Everyone wanted that gold watch for longevity. For good reasons, few spoke about early exit strategies and cashing out.

The agency under Abe Lastfogel and his immediate successors had fostered an image of trust and stability, plodding along more like the tortoise than the hare. The law of the jungle may have always been in play, but it had been cloaked in more civility than the open warfare that would become more commonplace in twenty-first-century workplaces. Like in a family, not everyone got along all the time, and conflicts and squabbles occurred, but there was an overriding sense of protection. It is that family feeling that former employees always cite as the biggest thing they miss from that time. It felt like a nostalgic relic from a quaint time in the past, like a once-cherished item at a garage sale, now viewed as nothing more than worthless junk.

There would have been no shame to call it a day. On the contrary, he would have exited in triumph. Within the walls of that company, he had accomplished everything he had set out to do. He had followed the same advice he often gave his children: "Do the best you can." He had set that same intention for himself and followed it to the letter every day. It worked both on a good day when everything went his way and helped him move on to find a new way when adversity blocked his path. In the end, he had accomplished all his goals in life and had succeeded in creating for himself a life of enormous accomplishment and gratification.

In many respects, Norman could be compared to an aging athlete who stayed on past his prime. As much as he embraced change as a natural and needed facelift for the company, he had a harder time with a more radical shift in the company's heart and soul. The almost naïve innocence that Marlo Thomas spoke about had a downside. It was a bitter pill to swallow, like a child's going out into the real world and suddenly learning that life is not fair.

It was telling that when Abe Lastfogel was in declining health, he still came into the office every day and followed the same routine of going to his desk to look at correspondence, having lunch, and watching a film in the screening room before retreating to his residence at the Beverly Wilshire. He was treated by all as the grand patriarch, and deservedly so, although he had little to say because his short-term memory was shot. But ask him what his private phone number or home address was in 1930, he didn't miss a beat. His was a long, loving farewell.

Norman had expected the same treatment. And to a good degree, he received it, especially from the rank and file. On the anniversary marking his sixtieth year at the company, everyone gathered in the lobby and gave him a standing ovation. But in truth he was like an aged but still proud stag being pushed into irrelevance, to the farthest margins of his herd. This was now the twenty-first century.

Perhaps the saving grace in it all was the power of the relationships he had developed over the many decades. How fortunate Norman was that he had clients who cared as much about him as he did about them and were not shy about telling him how much he meant to them. The last person I spoke with to complete the book was Priscilla Presley. It was so fitting, because she was the epitome of what made him so passionately dedicated to his work and the people he represented.

I can recall less than a handful of times when Norman allowed himself to be the center of attention in a public setting. One was a gathering to celebrate his eightieth birthday at Hillcrest Country Club. Almost all of his clients were there, and many spoke and performed in tribute, including Donna Summer's unforgettable rendition of "Someone to Watch Over Me."

Sitting next to Norman at his table was Priscilla. She did not need to speak, nor did she perform. She didn't have to, because her energy spoke volumes. She was seated in my direct line of sight. Throughout the entirety, she made it abundantly clear from the expression in her eyes how dearly she held him. And true to the occasion of an eightieth birthday, it was tinged with a sense of impermanence, marking the beginning of the unwelcome end of an era.

"Hollywood can be a very cruel place," she told me. "I knew that if anything or anyone made me feel uncomfortable, I could call him at any time, and he would always resolve it. If I was upset because they changed a script and put in something I didn't agree to, he would take care of it. He was very proud of what I was doing and encouraged me to explore new ventures. And I did so because I knew he was in my corner."

CHAPTER 28

The Rolodex

"I'M GOING TO THE OFFICE TOMORROW MORNING," NORMAN ANNOUNCED. It was his way of attempting to gain a sense of normalcy in an internal world turned completely upside down. The tomorrows would come and go, and Norman did not go into the office. His row of beautifully tailored suits hanging in the closet would remain untouched, the rack of colorful silky neckties and stacks of freshly laundered custom-made shirts similarly so.

It is said that the scourge of modern life is the likelihood of the mind deteriorating more quickly than the body. Advancements in medical treatments against cardiovascular disease that had decimated his family had extended life expectancy far beyond what his father, mother, and older brothers were given. Norman enjoyed the highest level of medical care available at the time. A quadruple bypass he received in the mid-1990s to deal with a 90 percent clogged widowmaker had plausibly given him another twenty years. But no drugs or surgery could deal with the plaque in the blood vessels of his brain that was slowly strangling his life force.

One cardiologist told me that cardiovascular disease was more of an impact of modern civilization, as if the human body was better engineered to deal with the feast-or-famine realities of caveman existence—not the "eat until we are stuffed" abundance and unhealthy choices and indulgences of modern society. From our primal roots, we are designed to be efficient hoarders of fat, since it is the best way to store energy for lean times—and some of that surplus fat clogs up our veins and arteries. It could also simply be that cavepeople rarely lived long enough to develop heart disease, let alone Alzheimer's and other forms of dementia.

Telling us that he was going to the office the next morning was a form of denial that almost everyone well advanced in the aging process experiences to varying degrees. None of us think that giving up our personal independence is a good thing. Neither do we want to appear to others to be in a vulnerable state. For someone in the agency business, this last aspect could become a kiss of death. Despite loyalty and longevity, clients may wonder if you are still up to the job and may start looking elsewhere. Competitors will gently (or not so gently) switch into vulture mode. Failure to come into the office in a timely fashion after a surgery or a bout with anything, and the red flags will start flapping in the wind. And soon they would.

"You live long enough, you get everything," Norman used to joke, and he was a living testimony to that fact. First, the quadruple heart bypass. Cataract surgery. Chunks of his face were periodically shaved off because of skin cancer. Carotid artery Roto-Rooter. Cancer in his throat area required surgery, radiation, and the implant of a gastric tube because of his difficulty swallowing. An infected gallbladder ruptured and nearly did him in.

With so much to attend to on the physical side, Marguerite did not isolate the cognitive decline in the sea of care issues he presented until it was becoming painfully obvious. "Oh, I have that picture in my house," he told her. He believed that he was not in his own home, and he wanted to go there. She heard from friends who had already been through it with a family member how it was a common, stereotypical sign.

Marguerite took him to see a geriatric psychiatrist, who recommended against conventional medications because of complications that might arise from his underlying health issues. After trying some of the natural remedies, like flower essences, the decision was made to use CBD, prescribed by a medical doctor specializing in cannabis treatment since it was not available at retail. Norman liked it, and for the time being it seemed to have a good effect.

In the same way he perseverated on going to the office, Norman continued as if everything were normal, hiding any sign to the contrary, not just with his few visitors and other family members but also with Marguerite. If she brought up concerns, he told her emphatically that he didn't want to talk about it. He insisted on having his set of keys in his man-purse always by his side because he said he wanted to drive again and talked about getting lessons to renew his license.

His ability to hold himself together was impressive as his condition worsened. In 2010, when the Academy of Television Arts & Sciences gave him the Governors Award, it turned out to be a perfect swan song to an industry and profession he loved. This award was truly reserved for industry pioneers like Walter Cronkite, Johnny Carson, Bob Hope, Lucille Ball, and CBS magnate William S. Paley. Never had a working agent ever held an Emmy statue with his name inscribed on it. The video introduction showing a montage of all the legendary programs he had shepherded reinforced how deserved this honor was. We as his family held our collective breaths, wondering if he was going to make it as he walked out on the stage and read his acceptance speech from a piece of paper in his hands. His voice was weak and hardly audible to the audience, but he made it through and received a standing ovation from his peers. For the rest of the event backstage, he would not let go of the heavy statue, fearing it would vanish if it left his grip.

As the months became years, the quality of his life progressively diminished. His world was shrinking to just the inside the four walls, venturing outside the home only for medical appointments. A chairlift was installed in the staircase, allowing him the run of the house, but soon it was no longer needed. In the confined space upstairs, he became increasingly restless, commuting between his bed and a stuffed chair in an adjacent study. Before long the physical strain of caring for him became too much for Marguerite alone. He required around-the-clock caregivers, which he abhorred. He had taken such immaculate care of his appearance from scalp to toenails, so he viewed it all as an indignity, a bitter pill signifying that he had lost control.

For someone who had such a gift of gab, he was also becoming increasingly silent. In the beginning he asked about Barbara every day. Then, suddenly, he quit, never to mention her name again. He stopped participating in everything except waking up for meals and going back to sleep. It became meaningless for close friends or colleagues to come to see him, since he had lost the ability to hold conversations. Afternoons and evenings were especially difficult due to sundowning. His behavior could become erratic, lashing out in anger that was totally uncharacteristic and polar opposite to who he had been.

Visits with him could be hit or miss, and mostly miss. For a good part of this time, I was living in New Hampshire and would fly out monthly to see him for a couple of days at a time. On one such visit, I noticed that Marguerite was not there. Norman had just awakened and his helper had moved him from the bed to his favorite upholstered chair. "Where's Marguerite," I asked him, not expecting any answer in return. "Oh, she's not here," he said as clear as a bell. "She and Bow (the miniature poodle) went to get their hair done." With a gentle smile, he added, "But they went to two separate places." He had loved telling bad jokes, and rising above the brain fog for a few moments with this little one, he was effectively telling me not to count him out yet.

A few months later, Norman was bedridden and needed to be transported by ambulance for an in-office procedure at his doctor's office. The ride there was bumpy, but his eyes remained closed as they jostled back and forth over the potholes. They had arrived early and were waiting in the hallway for probably a half hour. Again, Norman seemed oblivious, if not comatose. And then he opened his eyes. "What in hell is taking so long," he exclaimed with perfect comedic timing, to everyone's laughter.

It may sound weird, but my series of final visits with my father were extraordinarily precious to me. Whatever negativity I might have felt toward him because of his emotional distance and controlling nature during my upbringing evaporated. Despite the obvious suffering he was going through and the diminished communication, he was remarkably present, as if all the external trappings that had encased this powerhouse of a persona had withered away. For the first time, he was allowing me to see him at his core. I was seeing the beauty of the child he had once been—the one his cousin Mildred had witnessed and told me everything about.

After Norman passed away at home a few months short of his ninetieth birthday, on October 29, 2016, Mary Feinberg packed up what was left of his office, putting all the photos in the silver frames in moving boxes, along with other artifacts and mementos. One of the remaining objects on her desk was an enormous Rolodex. "It was the most incredible thing, really," Mary recalled. "It could have gone to the Smithsonian." Attached to its spindle were a few hundred small cards, containing not only names, addresses, and phone numbers but also personal data like birthdays, children's names, and much more. Each card told a story, and together they represented the hard-earned fruit of a life's work, of relationships nurtured, of deals made or lost, of lives intermingled with caring, generosity, and love. "It seemed like he knew everybody, like he was one degree of separation away from everybody on Earth." Thinking that the last thing he would have desired was for her to leave it behind, to potentially fall into someone else's hands, she packed it together with her belongings and took it home with her.

The Rolodex remained in her possession for two years, but it made her feel unsettled. "This is not what he would have wanted," Mary decided. One day, she took it out to her backyard, lit a match, and patiently watched the steady plume of smoke until the last card had turned to ash.

INDEX

Academy of Television Arts and Sciences, Governors Award from, 40, 185
Acapulco, 132
Adams, Nick, 56
Adidas, 127
AFTRA, 97
Ahbez, Eben, 104
Alex Hyde Orchestra, 10
Ali, Muhammad, 65
Allen, Woody, 156
Allenberg, Bert, 35; Young and, 37–38
American Idol, 45
Amos 'n Andy, 10
The Andy Griffith Show, Thomas, D., and, 71
Anheuser-Busch, 130
anti-semitism, 7
Arms, Frances. *See* Lastfogel, Frances
Armstrong, Louis, 170
Armstrong, Neil, 125
Arnaz, Desi, 37; Thomas, D., and, 70
Arnold, Eddie, 62
Auntie Mame, 123

"Bad Girls," 141
Ball, Lucille, 37, 185; Thomas, D., and, 70
Ball of Fire, 39
Bandini, Mario "Count," 54–55, 57
Banducci, Enrico, 156
Bankhead, Tallulah, 10
Barbara Graham (fictional character), 121
Barker, Tim, 122, 123–24
Bar Mitzvah, 21
Barnum, 150–51
Beach Boys, the, 64
Beatles, the, 64; Parker and, 63
Benny, Jack: Berner and, 77; at Hillcrest Country Club, 92
Berg, Jeff, 180
Berle, Milton, 36; at Hillcrest Country Club, 92; *Texaco Star Theater* with, 34
Berner, Sara, 76, 77, 78
Bernstein, Jay, 123
Betty Ford Center, 138, 139, 146–48, 152
The Big Valley, 39
Birch, Dean, 138

Bishop, Joey, 95–99, *96*
Bogart, Neil, 141
Bootzin, Robert (Gypsy Boots), 104–5
Bradley, Omar, 113
Brice, Fanny, 17; driving for, 26–27
Britton, Barbara, 35
Brokaw, Barbara (daughter), 114–19, 185; Brokaw, M., and, 161–62, 164, 165; at Kahala Hilton, *118*
Brokaw, Barbara (sister), 12–14
Brokaw, David (grandfather), 11
Brokaw, David (son), 28–29; with Brokaw, Suzane, 101–4, *104*; in Cadillac on Saturday, 80–82; car accident of, 82–83; with DiMaggio, 49, *50*; with family, *78*; with Wood and Wagner, 86
Brokaw, Donnie (brother), 12, *13*
Brokaw, Eddie (brother), *13*, 17; home movies of, 79; in World War II, 27
Brokaw, Florence (wife), *76*; divorce from, 101; with family, *78*; mental illness of, 51–52, 75–85
Brokaw, Irving (brother), 12, *13*; death of, 20; in World War II, 19–20
Brokaw, Isidore (father), 11–12, *18*; Brokaw, Barbara (sister), and, 14; death of, 17; stock market crash and, 15–16

Brokaw, Joel (son): with Brokaw, Suzane, 101–4, *104*; in Cadillac on Saturday, 80–82; car accident and, 82–83; with family, *78*; Jules and, 119; in swimming pool, 77; with Thomas, D., *74*; at Vick Place, 114; at Will Rogers State Beach, 131–32; with Wood and Wagner, 86
Brokaw, Lauren (daughter), 164, 165
Brokaw, Lenny (brother), *13*
Brokaw, Marguerite (wife), 161–67, *163*, 184–86
Brokaw, Marie (mother), *8, 9, 10, 11, 13*; Brokaw, Barbara (sister), and, 12–14; heart attack of, 20, 21; Hyde, J., and, 23–24; Ladies Athletic Club of, 17
Brokaw, Norman, *2, 13, 25*; with Bishop, *96*; with Brokaw, F., *76*; with Brokaw, M., *163*; with Brokaw, Suzane, *104*; with Cosby, B., *155*; with DiMaggio, *50*; fishing, *28*; with Ford, G., *136*; with Geffen, *110*; with Gordy, *172*; at Hillcrest Country Club, *93*; at Kahala Hilton, *118*; with Neimann-Legette, *147*; with Novak, K., *54*; with old guard, *178*; with Orlando, T., *151*; at Pennsylvania Drug Company, 17; with Prince Rainier, *133*; with Rockefellers, *134*; with

Spitz, M., *128*; with Summer,
143; with Thomas, D., *74*; with
Wagner, *88*; with Young, *38*. *See
also specific topics*
Brokaw, Rose (grandmother), 11
Brokaw, Sandy (son): with
Brokaw, Suzane, 101–4, *104*;
in Cadillac on Saturday, 80–82;
car accident and, 82–83; with
DiMaggio, 49, *50*; with family,
78; with Wood and Wagner, 86
Brokaw, Sidney (brother), 12, *13*;
World War II and, 20
Brokaw, Suzane "Sue" (wife),
102–5, *104*; abortion of, 115;
divorce from, 119; at Kahala
Hilton, *118*; OCD of, 114, 116;
at Vick Place, 114–19
Brokaw, Wendy (daughter),
114, 116–19, 164; at Kahala
Hilton, *118*
Brown Derby, 94; Monroe at,
45–52
Bruce, Lenny, 156
Buress, Hannibal, 154
Burke, Sam, 26
Burns, George, *29*; at Hillcrest
Country Club, 92

Cadillac on Saturday, 80–82
Caesar, Sid, 36
Caffe Roma, 94
Cameron, Sue, 166
"Candida," 149

Cantor, Eddie, 10; at Hillcrest
Country Club, 92; Holzman
and, 27
car accident, of Brokaw, David,
82–83
cardiovascular disease, 183–84
Carsey, Marcy, 158–59
Carson, Johnny, 97, 185
Carter, Jimmy, 132–33, 138
Casablanca Records, 141
Cedars-Sinai Medical Center, 92,
139, 152, 161–62, 179
Cheney, Dick, 135
Chiang Kai-shek, 113
chimpanzee: Bishop and, 97;
Lastfogel, A., and, 69–74
Christie, Agatha, 52
Chuck Webb Orchestra, 16
Cleveland, W. S., 9–10
Coca, Imogene, 36
Cohn, Harry, 53, 54–55
Cole, Nat King, 104, 170
Colgate Comedy Hour, 36
Columbia Pictures, 53–55
Coney Island, 15, 21
The Conqueror, 123
Cosby, Bill, 3, 153–60, *155*, 177
Cosby, Camille, 155, 156, 159
Cosby, Ennis, 153
The Cosby Show, 158–59, 163
Crawford, Joan, 37
Cronkite, Walter, 185
Culp, Robert, 157–58

Dale, Jim, 150

The Danny Thomas Show, 70–71
Darnell, Linda, 10
Davis, Bette, 37
Davis, Billy, Jr., 166
Davis, Sammy, Jr., 170; in Rat
    Pack, 95
Dean, James, 63
Death March of Bataan, 20
dementia, 65, 154, 184
Denver, John, 117, 132
De Sica, Vittorio, 43
Desilu Productions, 37
Diana Ross and the
    Supremes, 169
The Dick Van Dyke Show, Thomas,
    D., and, 71
A Different World, 159
DiMaggio, Joe, *50*; Monroe and,
    49–50
"Dim All the Lights," 141–
    42, 144
Double Indemnity, 39
driver's license, 26–27
Durante, Jimmy: Lastfogel, A.,
    and, 69; Thomas, D., and, 74

Eagels, Jeanne, 57
Eastwood, Clint, 3, 41–42, *42*; at
    Hillcrest Country Club, *93*
Elvis, 61
Epstein, Brian, 63

Feinberg, Mary, 5–6, 165–66,
    186–87; on Bishop, 95
Fellini, Federico, 43

Fifth Dimension, The, 166
fishing, *28*, 28–29
Fistful of Dollars, 43
Fitzgerald, Ella, 16
Ford, Betty, 132, 137–38, 162;
    Betty Ford Center and, 138,
    139, 146–48, 152; Orlando, T.,
    and, 150
Ford, Gerald, 3, 132–33, 135–39,
    136, 162; Orlando, T., and, 150
Four Tops, the, 169
Foxx, Jimmie, 49
Frawley, Bill, 48–49
Fred Mertz (fictional charac-
    ter), 48
From Here to Eternity, 53
Furie, Sidney, 171

Gable, Clark, 50; Young and, 41
Gabor, Zsa Zsa, 33; Schechter
    and, 61
Gale, Robert, 145
Garland, Judy, 16
Gaye, Marvin, 169
Geffen, David, 1–7, *110*
Gehrig, Lou, 16
Gladys Knight and the Pips, 169
Goetz, Bill, 24
Goldwyn, Samuel, 92
Goldwyn Studios, 39
Gomer Pyle, U.S.M.C., 71
Goodwin, Les, 35
Gordy, Berry, 3, 169–73, *172*

Governors Award, from Academy
of Television Arts and Sciences,
40, 185
Gray, Coleen, 35
Greenberg, Hank, 49
Greenson, Ralph, 52
Gregory, Dick, 156
Gurdin, Maria, 85–86
Gypsy Boots (Robert Bootzin),
104–5

Hadley, Reed, 35
"The Haidabura Troupe," 9–10
Haig, Alexander, 138
Hammer, Armand, 138, 145
Hanks, Tom, 61
Hart to Hart, 85
Hawn, Goldie, 117
Hayward, Susan, 3, 121–24, *122*
Hayworth, Rita, 10
Heat of Anger, 123
"He Don't Love You (Like I Love
You)," 149
Hendricks, Wanda, 35
Henie, Sonja, 126
Hepburn, Katherine, 37
Hillcrest Country Club, 91–94,
93, 166, 182
Hirshan, Lenny, 41
Hitchcock, Alfred, 77
Holiday, Billie, 171
Holzman, Ben, 27–28
Hope, Bob, 10, 185
"Hot Stuff," 141
Hughes, Howard, 113

Hutton, Betty, 10
Hyde, Alex, *8*, 8–9, 10
Hyde, Johnny, 9, 10–11, 23–26;
Brokaw, Marie, and, 23–24;
death of, 48; Monroe and,
46–48, *47*; Williams, E.,
and, 56
Hyde, Nettie, *8*, 8–9, 10
Hyde, Nicholas, *8*, 8–9, 10
Hyde, Olga, *8*, 8–9
Hyde, Rosa (grandmother), *8*,
8–9, 23
Hyde, Victor, *8*, 8–9, 10

ICM, 150, 180
I Love Lucy, 37; Frawley on, 48;
Thomas, D., and, 70
IMG, 126
International Pictures, 24
Interview, 41
I Spy, 157–58
It's a Wonderful Life, 70
I Want to Live, 121

Jackson, Autumn, 153
Jackson, Calvin, *29*
Jackson Five, the, 169
Jaws, 129
Jessel, George, 10; at Hillcrest
Country Club, 92; Holzman
and, 27
Jolson, Al, 10; Holzman and, 27
Jordan, Michael, 127
Jules (family helper), 118–19, 165

Kahala Hilton, 117–19, *118*, 132, *133*, *134*
Kaye, Danny, 92
Kelly, Grace, 117, 132
Kennedy, Bobby, 114
Kennedy, John F., 97, 133
Khan, Aly (Prince), 56
kidney stones, 139
King, Martin Luther, Jr., 113, 169, 170
Knight, Gladys, 169
"Knock Three Times," 149
Koop, C. Everett, 138–39
Korngold, Erich, 10
Kroc, Ray, 113
Kuchel, Thomas, 113, 164

La Cortigiana di Babilonia, 43
Ladies Athletic Club, of Brokaw, Marie (mother), 17
The Lady Eve, 39
Lady Sings the Blues, 171
Landis, Lou, 35
Landon, Michael, 117
Lansbury, Angela, 123
La Scala, 94
Lastfogel, Abe, 10, 31–36, *32*, 53–54, *178*, 180; chimpanzee and, 69–74; Durante and, 69; family visit with, 81–82; at Hillcrest Country Club, 92–93; Novak, K., and, 53–54; Parker and, 62, 63; portrait of, *176*; Presley, E., and, 59; Thomas, D., and, 70–74; at Will Rogers State Beach, 131; Wood and Wagner with, 85
Lastfogel, Frances, 62, 70–71, *74*; family visit with, 81–82; at Hillcrest Country Club, 92–93; at Will Rogers State Beach, 131; Wood and Wagner with, 85
Lawford, Patricia Kennedy, 97
Lawford, Peter, 95, 97
Lazar, Swifty, 138
Lemmon, Jack, 117
Leonard, Sheldon, 70, 72, 149; Cosby, B., and, 156, 157
Leone, Sergio, 43
Levi, Carol, 41–43
Lewis, Judy, 41
Lewis, Tom, *38*
Libby, Mildred, 14
Lidén, Tom, 65
Life Magazine, 142
Lights, Camera, Action, 45
Liston, Sonny, 65
Litke, Marty, 156
Loews Vaudeville Circuit, 10
Longley, Marguerite. *See* Brokaw, Marguerite
The Loretta Young Show, 39
Los Angeles Times, 132, 136
Louis, Joe, *29*
Luau, The, 57
Lynn, Diana, 35

Mabel Flapsaddle (fictional character), 77

MacArthur, Douglas, 19
Make Room for Daddy, 70–71
Martha and the Vandellas, 169
Martin, Dean, 95
Marx, Chico, 10, 92
Marx, Groucho, 10, 92
Marx, Harpo, 10, *29*; at Hillcrest Country Club, 92
Mayer, Louis B., 92
McCoo, Marilyn, 166
McCormack, Mark, 126–27
McQueen, Steve, 72
#MeToo, 154
MGM, 24, 45; Montalban and, 43
Mitchell, Frank, 35
The Mod Squad, 71
money, 80
Monroe, Marilyn, 3, 171; at Brown Derby, 45–52; death of, 52; DiMaggio and, 49–50; Hyde, J., and, 46–48, *47*; plastic surgery of, 46; Presley, E., and, 60–61
Montalban, Ricardo, 43
Moore, Terry, 113
Morris, William, *176*
Motown, 169–73
Mouse in the Rat Pack (Starr), 98–99
Mr. and Mrs. North, 35
Munao, Susan, 141
My Little Margie, 36
"My Sweet Gypsy Rose," 149

Nathan's hot dogs, 15, 21

"Nature Boys," 104
Neimann-Legette, Nansci, 146–48, *147*
New York World's Fair, 34
Nike, 127
Nixon, Richard, 132, 133, 138; "Enemies List" of, 154–55
"No More Tears/Enough Is Enough," 141, 144
Novak, Adam, 5, *54*
Novak, Kim, 1–2, 53–58, 166, 171; Lastfogel, A., and, 53–54; in *Man with the Golden Arm*, 53

O'Brien, Hugh, 56
Orlando, Rhonda, 150
Orlando, Tony, 149–51, *151*; Parker and, 66–67
Our Gang, 102
Ozzie Nelson Orchestra, 12

Paley, William S., 185
Palm Desert, 164
Parade, 27
Paramount Studios, 23, 43
Parker, Tom (Colonel), 57–67, *60*; the Beatles and, 63; counting the house by, 62; Lastfogel, A., and, 62, 63; as negotiator, 62–63; Orlando, T., and, 66–67; Presley, E., and, 59–67; Schechter and, 61–64
Pennsylvania Drug Company, 16–17, *17*
Penny, Don, 133–38

Perry, Tyler, 71
Phelps, Michael, 125
Philbin, Regis, 97–98
Phil Brokaw (fictional charac-
    ter), 71
Phillips, Sam, 62
piano lessons, 16
Power, Tyrone, 41
Presley, Elvis, 3; the Beatles and,
    63; Monroe and, 60–61; Parker
    and, 59–67; Streisand and, 63
Presley, Priscilla, 61, 63, 65,
    67, 182
Prinze, Freddie, 150
Procter & Gamble, 138–39
product licensing, 127
Public Defender, 36
"Put It in Writing," at William
    Morris Agency, 46

Racket Squad, 35, 36
Rainier (Prince), 117, 132, *133*
Rat Pack, 95–97, 98–99
Rawhide, 41
Rawls, Lou, 131
Reagan, Ronald, 135
The Real McCoys, 71
Rear Window, 77
"The Rebel," 56
Reddy, Helen, 152
Rittenband, Laurence, 162
Ritz Brothers, 10
Rivers, Joan, 156
Rivkin, Joe, 102–3, 104
Robinson, Edward D., 74

Robinson, Smokey, 169
Rockefeller, Happy, 132, *134*
Rockefeller, Nelson, 132, *134*
Rolling Stones, the, 64
Rolodex, 187
Romanoff's, 94
Rooney, Mickey, 10, 16
Roseanne, 159
Ross, Diana, 169, 171
Rowan & Martin's Laugh-In, 3
Rowdy Yates (fictional charac-
    ter), 41
Ruth, Babe, 49

Salomon, Lee, 102
Saturday Night Review, 36
Schechter, Irv, 33; Gabor and, 61;
    Parker and, 61–64
Schlatter, George, 3; on
    Bishop, 98
Schlosser, Herb, 157
Schoenfeld, Joe, *178*
Schwartz, Alan, 110–12
Scott, Walter, 27
Screen Actors Guild, 46
"The 700 Club," 66
Shearer, Lloyd, 27
The Sheik, 37
Shields, Brooke, 3
The Show of Shows, 36
signature knock, 57
Sinatra, Frank, *29*; Anheuser-
    Busch and, 130; Bishop and,
    98; in *From Here to Eternity*, 53;
    at Hillcrest Country Club, 94;

in *Man with the Golden Arm*,
53; Parker and, 63; Rat Pack of,
95–97; records of, 64
Skelton, Red, *29*
Smokey Robinson and the
Miracles, 169
Smothers Brothers, the, 156
The Snake Pit, 76
Snow, Hank, 62
Some Like It Hot, 10
"Someone to Watch Over Me,"
144, 182
Spago, 94, 166
Spelling, Aaron, 71; Thomas, D.,
and, 74
Spelling, Candy, *74*
Spielberg, Steven, 129
Spitz, Arnold, 125
Spitz, Leo, 24
Spitz, Leonore, 125
Spitz, Mark, 3, 125–30, *128*, 137;
at Hillcrest Country Club, *93*,
93–94
Splendor in the Grass, 86
Stanwyck, Barbara, 3, 39–40, 123
A Star Is Born, 63
Starr, Michael Seth, 98–99
Stella Dallas, 39
Stern, 126
stock market crash, 15–16
Stoller, Morris, 177, *178*
Streisand, Barbra, 63; Litke and,
156; Summer and, 141
The Stu Erwin Show, 36

Summer, Donna, 3, 141–44, *143*,
161, 182
Sun Records, 62
Supremes, the, 169
Survivor, 175

A Talent for People (Brokaw, N.), 3,
4, 5, 148
Tarzan, 126
Temptations, the, 169
ten day wonders, 35
Texaco Star Theater, 34
That Girl, 71
This Year's Blonde, 46
Thomas, Danny, 3, *74*; Bishop
and, 97; driving for, 26–27;
at Hillcrest Country Club,
92; Lastfogel, A., and, 70–74;
Leonard and, 70–71, 72, 149;
on Vick Place, 113
Thomas, Marlo, 71, 72; on
Hillcrest Country Club, 92
"Tie a Yellow Ribbon 'Round the
Ole Oak Tree," 149–50
To Have and Have Not, 70
Tony Orlando and Dawn, 150
Tracy, Spencer, 50; Young and, 41
Truman, Harry, 137
Tucker, Sophie, 17
Turner, Lana, 10
20th Century Fox, 48

USO: Monroe at, 50; in
World War II, 31–33

Valentino, Rudolph, 37
Van Dyke, Dick, 3, 152
Vick Place, 113–19

The Wackiest Ship in the Army, 135
Wagner, Robert, *88*; Wood,
    Natalie and, 85–89
Wald, Jeff, 152
Wallis, Hal, 63
Warner, Jack, 92
Warner Brothers, 23, 43
Waxman, Franz, 10
Wayne, John, 123
Weinberger, Caspar, 138
Weintraub, Suzane "Sue." *See*
    Brokaw, Suzane
Weisbord, Sam, 131, 162, 165–66,
    177, *178*
Weissmuller, Johnny, 126
Werner, Mort, 157
Werner, Tom, 158–59
West, Mae, 10
Weston, Jay, 171
West Side Story, 86
Whiteman, Paul, 10
Wide World of Sports, 126
William Morris Agency, 1; chair-
    man and CEO of, 164; changes

at, 175–82; IMG and, 126;
    internship at, 114; mailroom of,
    107–12, *110*; offices of, 81; "Put
    It in Writing" at, 46; radio at,
    36; television at, 33–43. *See also*
    specific individuals and topics
Williams, Esther, 24; Hyde, J.,
    and, 56
Williams, Hank, 62
Will Rogers State Beach, 131–32
Wonder, Stevie, 169
Wood, Natalie, 3, 72, *87*; as
    businesswoman, 142; Wagner,
    Robert, and, 85–89
World War II: Brokaw, E., in,
    27; Brokaw, Irving, in, 19–20;
    Brokaw, Sidney, and, 20; USO
    Camp Shows in, 31–33
"Wyatt Earp," 56

Young, Loretta, 3, 37–39, *38*;
    as businesswoman, 142; date
    rape of, 41; leading men of, 41;
    swear box of, 40

Zifkin, Walt, 53
Zukor, Adolph, 92, 93–94

ACKNOWLEDGMENTS

Heartfelt thanks go first and foremost to Chris Enss and her unswerving conviction that Norman's story needed to be told. She put me in touch with her publisher and editor, Rick Rinehart, who saw historical value and appeal in this peak behind the curtains of the dream factory. But it all began with the magic touch of my brother David Brokaw, who took the initiative to share with Chris some of my writings of classic Norman anecdotes. And a big thank-you to David Geffen for contributing the foreword and crystalizing for us what made Norman so remarkable and unforgettable.

This book would not have materialized without the eager and enthusiastic participation of so many. It was a loving testament to the wonderful relationships Norman nurtured during his lifetime that everyone generously made time in their busy lives to speak with me. The list is long, beginning with Norman's colleagues Walt Zifkin and Irv Schecter and his longtime assistant, Mary Feinberg. Clients like Kim Novak, Tony Orlando, Mark Spitz, Berry Gordy, Robert Wagner, Priscilla Presley, George Schlatter, and Marilyn McCoo and Billy Davis Jr. gave me a wealth of material. Colleagues including Nansci Neimann-Legette (who many years earlier had urged Norman to tell his story), Susan Munao, Sue Cameron, Alan Schwartz, and Tim Barker shared invaluable insights.

Last but hardly least, I had the best sounding boards, fact checkers, and cheerleaders in my immediate family: my brothers Sandy and David Brokaw, sisters Wendy Brokaw Kretchmer and Lauren Brokaw, son (and consummate family historian) Nicholas Brokaw, and daughter Julia Brokaw, who were both always happy to jump in when I needed help on anything. Stepmother Marguerite Brokaw's contributions were invaluable, as both an interview subject and a sounding board. She understood better than any of us what made Norman tick.

Hugs of gratitude must be given to my wife, Birte, for putting up with me. A book project is not much different from an unruly houseguest who long overstays his welcome.